THE WAR WITHIN

THE WALDEMAR LEONHARDT STORY

AS TOLD TO MORGAN VOGEL CHINNOCK

Pacific Press® Publishing Association
Nampa, Idaho
Oshawa, Ontario, Canada
www.pacificpress.com

Cover design by Steve Lanto
Cover design resources from www.dreamstime.com and
www.iStockphoto.com
Inside photos provided by Waldemar Leonhardt
Inside design by Aaron Troia

The author assumes full responsibility for the accuracy of all facts and
quotations as cited in this book. Some names have been changed to
protect individuals' privacy. All translations by Waldemar Leonhardt
unless otherwise noted.

Bible quotations are from the New King James Version (NKJV)
copyright © 1979, 1980, 1982, Thomas Nelson, Inc., Publishers.

You can obtain additional copies of this book by calling toll-free
1-800-765-6955 or by visiting http://www.adventistbookcenter.com.

ISBN 13: 978-0-8163-2374-6
ISBN 10: 0-8163-2374-7

09 10 11 12 13 • 5 4 3 2 1

For Udo, Nora, Edmund, and Rhonda

Acknowledgments

I thank Waldemar for courageously telling his story and trusting me to help him share it. I also thank

- Lynne Thew, Cynthia Westerbeck, and Ric Henry for lending their eyes, hearts, and experience;
- my parents, Bart and Debra, my brother Max, Jaymie de la Torre, and Rachel Fox for testing this story and cheering me on;
- John McDowell, who, besides vision and an intuitive eye on this project, has shared with me many tools a writer needs to walk in this world—particularly faith, fewer "be" verbs, dark chocolate, and grace;
- and always, my husband, Andy, who holds my hand as we both seek our adventures, believes in my dream and my pen, and did the dishes so we wouldn't end up eating on hubcaps.

—Morgan Vogel Chinnock

Contents

CHAPTER ONE — *On the Battleship*

9

CHAPTER TWO — *The Family Room*

21

CHAPTER THREE — *The Revolver*

34

CHAPTER FOUR — *Frozen in Escape*

48

CHAPTER FIVE — *Hunger*

57

CHAPTER SIX — *The Violin*

72

CHAPTER SEVEN — *Stuck in Reverse*

85

CHAPTER EIGHT — *American Dreams*

98

CHAPTER NINE — *Desert Nightmare*

112

CHAPTER TEN — *Father's Son*

123

CHAPTER ELEVEN — *The Living Room*

137

CHAPTER TWELVE — *On the Bridge*

147

EPILOGUE

155

PHOTOGRAPHS

158

CHAPTER ONE

On the Battleship

"Too bad your smile doesn't match the lovely sun, bloke!"

The British bus driver grins at me as he hands me my change. I nod but do not smile, and move toward the back of the bus. All day, the British have jabbered joyfully about the uncommonly sunny day. The sun seems to make their dry humor burst into bloom, but I always answer them with a scowl. Other than that, I must look like any other tourist, but I don't feel like one.

On this, my second trip back to Europe since the end of World War II, I thought it was finally time that I visit England. It has been fifty-four years since the war ended.

Before I arrived here in London, I wanted to see the famous city. I planned to get to know it by spending five days in it before traveling to my brother's home in Germany. But now that I'm here, I hate it.

The bus rides today have kept me standing, holding onto the cold overhead bar and trying not to touch the people around me. Although there are many tourists in the buses, I somehow always get stuck next to people who speak with a British accent, and I try extra hard not to brush against them. Spaniards, Chinese, Americans—I wouldn't mind bumping into them, but the British I cannot stand.

A very small grandmother in a flowered dress stands next to me on this ride. She holds a grocery bag in one hand and a little girl's hand in the other. Her granddaughter chatters the whole ride without taking a breath, and I see out of the corner of my eye that the grandmother, whose head is dangerously close to my hovering elbow, looks at me once in a while, hoping to catch my eye and wink about the little girl's endless chatter. I don't meet her eyes, but stare instead straight ahead—through the crowd of people—at the middle of the windshield, focusing intently on nothing in particular.

The bus lurches to a stop, and a potato falls out of the grandmother's grocery bag and lands at my feet. She must assume I'm a gentleman because at first she doesn't move. But I remain still, and so she bends over to get it. Her forearm brushes my shin as she stands up, and I feel a sudden chill run up my leg. It tingles the same way my forearms do when people scratch their nails on a chalkboard. "Sorry, deary," she says.

I watch her herd her pigtailed granddaughter down the bus steps, and the place where she touched me feels dirty. Even two bus stops later, I feel that spot on my shin as if it were separate from the rest of my body—the way my hand feels when I think it might have brushed poison ivy and I must quarantine it from every other part of me.

I suppose it is an uncommonly sunny day in London. The late afternoon air is warm as I step off the bus outside the Tower of London. I will visit the inside tomorrow, but I want to see the Tower Bridge today. White wisps of clouds float against a sky as bright as the bridge's blue cables when I look up from the street to snap a photo, probably only my fifth one today.

Usually, I am the first to strike up a conversation with a stranger, but all day I have shrunk from the people around me. I didn't expect this. I've lived in America for forty-three years now—I've been an American longer than I was a German citizen. I don't hate the Americans. More than that, I've been a Seventh-day Adventist for seven years. Why can I not feel love for these people? It is 1999, but ever since yesterday, when I stepped into Heathrow Airport, I have felt like it is 1944, and I am in the enemy's camp. Even when the blue eyes of that granddaughter on the bus flashed up at me, I saw the eyes of a killer—of a miniature soldier whose every thought was bent against my happiness.

All day, I have wandered, from Big Ben to Westminster Abbey to the British Museum, but I haven't really taken in the sights. I can't enjoy them. This is strange behavior for me. Even such a simple sight as abundant wildflowers in Colorado in March can capture me, and I can use a whole roll of film in three vista stops. But here, I have clicked only a few snapshots of the things I know people expect one to see on a visit to London.

After the required snapshot of the Tower Bridge, I put my hands in my pockets and walk slowly onto the bridge. A family walking toward me from the middle of the bridge catches my eye. It is a husband and wife swinging their toddler between them, each grasping one arm and swinging her as she giggles. They are completely absorbed in her laughter. As they near me, I look at the young father's face, notice the glint of the ring on his left hand, and I hate him. To me, that ring—that symbol of his belonging to a family—is despicable. Each family in England is a breeding machine for more soldiers, more enemies, more destroyers.

Tommy. That's what he is. That's what we called the English during the war. It is the word for the enemy—for those we must defeat, for those who, in the end, took our pride from us. I watch this young father, the sun washing out his white face, and I imagine him with a steel helmet on his forehead, a cigarette dangling from his mouth, a gun on his shoulder. The image fits perfectly. These people all seem innocent at home with their families, but deep down they are killing machines.

As the family nears me, the man looks out to the river, and his gaze passes quickly over my face on its way back to his daughter's. *Coward!* I spit the word out in my mind. He can't even make eye contact with me. *Coward. They're all cowards.*

I know, deep down somewhere, that these thoughts aren't completely true—that boys and girls from anywhere in the world are just boys and girls, and families anywhere in the world are families. But all I can see today is that all these people are enemies bent on destroying me. All of them. This is what I was taught as a child. "They" are the enemy. "They" are our oppressors. "They" must be defeated. And "they" meant everyone but the Aryan Germans.

I'm in the center of the bridge now, and, like a good tourist, I lean casually on the railing. The sun is lowering in the sky, and its rays catch the waves on the Thames, creating a choir of flashes in the water.

I force myself to continue to face the river, but I feel the Tommies walking behind me—the tiny Tommies-in-training, the female Tommies walking arm-in-arm with those men, so proud of their country. I don't feel safe. I don't want to stand with my back to them. My heart pounds in my chest, preparing me to run. They are monsters. They aren't like me.

Still, even with this heavy sickness in my stomach and this awareness of enemies around me, I will my feet to stay. Though I can't seem to focus on anything, my eyes stop at a tall sonar tower I see down the river. It belongs to a battleship—a battleship whose guns are pointed directly at me. I shake my head. My brother Erwin was killed on a ship in the English Channel. Something from deep down in the middle of the knot of hate in my stomach rises to the surface, and suddenly my eyes are cloudy with tears. My oldest brother, Erwin, was killed by the cowards on one of those ships.

My feet start to move. They take me over the bridge, toward the dock the battleship is tied to. During the five-minute walk, I alternate between deep sorrow and intense anger. When I pass a smartly dressed businessman on the sidewalk, all I can think is *coward, coward, coward.*

When no one is close to me, I swallow the growing ache in my throat—the ball of silenced sobs, and tears fill my eyes and blur them. I manage to raise my head enough to keep the tears from spilling over, but I keep my eyes half open so I see only the feet of the people passing me. They killed my brother.

They killed my four brothers.

There were seven of us to begin with. Six boys and one girl. I am the youngest.

Our family lived in a town far away from this island, far from the sea, in the forests of eastern Germany, in the region of Silesia, in the town Sprottau, named for the river Sprotte. *Sprottau.* The word feels good on my tongue. But now, even that word has changed. Ever since the town became part of Poland, it's been *Szprotawa.*

On the sidewalk, the click of high heels, the squeak of tennis shoes, the padding of leather loafers pass me. To me it is all a steady thudding, the pounding march of boots.

Sprottau was my world. And then it fell apart. Not all at once. The change sort of crept up on us. Late in 1938, Manfred, my closest brother in age, and I were running errands for Mama in town, and on our way to the dairy store we passed the shoe store. The windows were broken out, glass lying on the sidewalk, and the window display gone. Inside, I saw only three shoes left—one pair and a lonely boot—and they were smashed, as if many feet had trampled them. On the door was painted the word *Juden,* and a large *X* crossed it out.

We ran home past the broken windows of the clothing store. "Mama, Mama!" We told her everything, and she didn't say much at all. She just nodded her head as though she already knew. That was the beginning.

I am nearing the battleship. It is reappearing from behind a building. I don't know why I am still walking, why I even consider stepping on one of their ships. I blink, and a couple tears roll onto my cheeks.

After the Jews' stores were destroyed, I didn't think much more about Jews as individuals. The adults around me made jokes about them, and we even put on plays at school that made the Jews look like fools. In 1940, when I was ten years old, I was sworn into *Jungvolk,* the division of Hitler Youth—*Hitler Jugend*—for young boys and girls. I thrived on the marching and the patriotic songs. Erwin, my oldest brother, had volunteered for the navy in 1938. My other brothers were drafted quickly once they were old enough: Kurt and Walter in 1941, and Edmund in 1942. My fifty-four-year-old father was drafted as an officer in 1943, and Manfred was not quite sixteen when he was called into service in 1944. That made six Leonhardt men in the war.

Though Erwin was the first to go into military service, he wasn't the first to die. A few months after Kurt and Walter were drafted, we received notice that Walter was missing in action on the Russian front and presumed dead. I remember the evening when we got the letter. I was twelve. Edmund was at his dairy apprenticeship, and Manfred and I were at home with Mama and Papa.

It was a telegram. I was slopping the pigs when the postmaster brought it to the house. Manfred yelled to me from the back porch. The tone in his voice made me drop the bucket and come running, and when I entered the kitchen, Papa tore the envelope open.

While he read the telegram out loud, I watched Mama. She was drying her hands on her apron. A small woman, she usually set her mouth in a straight line with slightly upturned corners. Now, her mouth opened slightly, as though she needed more air. Her face went white. As Papa read, she stooped over the slightest bit, as though she had been punched gently in the stomach. When Papa finished, the top of her body rocked forward before her feet began to move. She didn't meet any of our eyes.

I followed her to the bedroom and stood at the door, my arms hanging at my sides. She knelt down and sobbed, and "Thank You, Lord," came out of her throat with every sob. "Thank You, Lord."

Every week of my childhood, she referred at least once to the story of Job—the part where Job says, "The Lord gave, and the Lord has taken away; blessed be the name of the Lord." She knew the Bible well, she was a good Lutheran, and even this news about Walter couldn't make her forget. "Thank You, Lord." It came in different volumes and pitches with her sobs, but that was her refrain.

I stood there while she prayed, "Thank You, Lord." My brother had died. "Thank You, Lord." They never found his body. "Thank You, Lord."

I couldn't understand. I was at the door, and she knelt on the other side of the bed. My eyes lost focus. The room blurred. I turned and walked slowly away. I was twelve years old.

My mother was resigned. She was sad about what had happened, but she couldn't do anything about it. I never heard her ask, "Why, God? Why him?"

We went to church that Sunday, and, just like every other Sunday, the pastor read the register of those who died in the war. He stood up high behind the pulpit, and the people stood below him, the men stoic, the children motionless, the more emotional women stifling sobs. He always said the same words: *"Fuer Fuehrer, Volk, und Vaterland,"* which means "For our leader, our people, and our fatherland."

"Fuer Fuehrer, Volk, und Vaterland: Artur Lieder."

"Fuer Fuehrer, Volk, und Vaterland: Gottfried Bauer."

"Fuer Fuehrer, Volk, und Vaterland: Mattias Koch."

"Fuer Fuehrer, Volk, und Vaterland: Walter Leonhardt."

Every Sunday, the scene recurred because there was always another soldier—or two or three or four—killed.

"Fuer Fuehrer, Volk, und Vaterland: Nicolaus Krueger."

"Fuer Fuehrer, Volk, und Vaterland: Friedrich Werner."

Our training—the patriotic songs they taught us to sing— told us that it was admirable to have a brother killed in the war. I don't recall experiencing any special feelings of sadness or anger. It was an honor. My sorrow and anger today are the strongest they've ever been, perhaps made so by being buried more than fifty years. Then, we knew my brother was not coming back, and we just accepted it. The adults didn't try to explain things to us or comfort us—"Maybe he's just missing. He'll come back." No, it was just "He's dead."

At least we received letters announcing Walter's and Erwin's deaths. Once Edmund and Manfred left to fight on the Russian front, we never heard from them or about them again. They just disappeared into the wreckage.

My vision is blurred now—the tears are strong. I fight them back, but I know my face is distorted from the effort. I swallow a lump in my throat, feel the ache deep in my chest, wish I could have known my brothers better so I would know what I was missing when they died.

I want a safe place to cry, a place I never knew as a child, but there are only shoes pounding on the sidewalk. I glance up and see a face, the face of a man about my age—late sixties—with about the same amount of hair fringing his bald scalp. He carries a loaf of bread. I realize he was here too—on this island when Erwin sank beneath the waves. *Murderer!* The word leaps to my throat but doesn't escape. *Murderers.* They murdered my brother. *He* murdered my brother. Enemies swarm around me.

Walter, Erwin, Edmund, Manfred. Four brothers killed, and we only knew for sure what happened to Erwin. A telegraph operator on a minesweeper, he sank to the bottom of the English Channel—the only grave I can point to. And so he comes to represent them all. Here, on this island, I meet the people who killed him, put a face to the enemy who killed *them,* all four of them—the brothers I never truly knew. I was eight, twelve, thirteen, and fourteen years old when he, he, he, and he left. The British water holds his body.

Then I'm beside the battleship. A queue has formed outside the ticket booth, and without really knowing why, I go to the end. I take off my glasses and rub my eyes as any old man will do at the end of a long day of sightseeing. By the time I have cleaned my glasses, I am at the booth and handing over my six pounds to board the ship. The man hands me a pamphlet with letters at the top that read HMS *Belfast*. It closes at six o'clock— I have only an hour. I wander down the ramp to the ship and manage to keep myself composed as I pass families scattered across the main deck.

I find a sign that points to deck two and descend a metal stair-case, turning sideways to fit in the narrow space. I have never been inside a battleship, and it strikes me that Erwin's ship must have looked a lot like this. On the mess deck there are tables with bench seats, and hammocks hang above the tables. Every inch of space is used. It is a dingy room with no natural light, only electric bulbs. In the hammocks and on the benches of the *Belfast,* there are wax mannequins in uniform. One of them sits in the corner reading a magazine. His face looks fake, but an-other dummy, wearing a naval cap, sits with his back to me, and I can almost imagine him breathing. My fists tighten.

I make my way quickly to the bottom deck and work my way back up. I pass through the magazine room, where there are rows and rows of cubbyholes for ammunition. Another weapons room holds the shells for the six-inch gun turrets. The shells that once tore holes in the hulls of ships are arranged in a circle, red tips pointed out, so no matter where I stand in the room, I cannot escape their aim.

In the wheelhouse, two mannequins helm the ship; one has bent over to adjust a valve. I stand behind them with fists clenched at my sides. I want to tell them something. I want to make them go away, to make them stop steering. The sorrow I have been fighting turns into a rage inside my chest. But the sailors don't move. They're dummies. What good would it do to pummel or yell at a mannequin?

Then I enter the telegraph room. This was where Erwin worked on his ship. An engineer, he sat right where that dummy now sits and decoded the Enigma messages that came over the airwaves. I wish he were sitting there. I stand here for a long time. I want him to be here. I would like to know him.

"Fuer Fuehrer, Volk, und Vaterland: Erwin Leonhardt."

Erwin. My oldest brother. My role model. When we got the letter about him, Mama didn't even sob, at least not when I could see her. Papa had been drafted into the army in 1943, so Mama opened the letter. I read it only after she laid it quietly on the table and left the room.

Paul Woldmann   Current Location
Lieutenant at Sea and Group Leader   March 15, 1944
Field Station Number M 19361

Dear Mr. Leonhardt,

I have the sad duty to inform you that your dear son, radio operator Lance Corporal Erwin Leonhardt, born on March 22, 1919, did not return from a sea battle in the English Channel. He has been declared missing in action as of March 14, 1944, 2200 hours. But, considering the outcome of the battle, there is no doubt that your dear son found his grave in the waters of the English Channel.

All of us, superiors and comrades of your dear son alike, are deeply saddened by the tragic loss and send you and your family our heartfelt condolences.

As radio operator, your dear son carried a heavy responsibility. Because of his tireless efforts and his excellent abilities, he met all challenges successfully and was highly respected. Among his comrades he was very much liked because of his calm demeanor.

On March 18, 1944, in the afternoon, several bodies recovered from the sea will be buried in the military cemetery at Stune near Ostende. Your son and the other missing comrades will also receive their last rites with military honors there.

Lastly, dear Mr. Leonhardt, I would ask you to send us a picture of your dear son, so it can receive a place of honor in the squadron's Camaraderie Hall.

Let me express my sincere personal sympathy for you and your family.

Heil Hitler,
Paul Woldmann, Lieutenant at Sea and Group Leader[*]

Fuer Fuehrer, Volk, und Vaterland, blessed be the name of the Lord. The Lord gave, the Lord has taken away, blessed be the name . . .
Fuer Fuehrer, Volk, the Lord has taken . . .
The Lord has taken . . .
The Lord has taken . . .
Blessed be the name of the Lord.

[*] Translated by Helmut Stutz.

CHAPTER TWO

The Family Room

My childhood was full of contradictions. In church—we were Lutherans—I heard about a God who gave great blessings, but who just as frequently took them away. I lived in a country that touted each citizen's superiority and right to rule the world and then called it an honor when we were slaughtered for its causes. But nothing was as contradictory as the view of God my family gave me as a child.

My parents' first child was a girl—Elfriede—but since only boys were born after her, Papa joked that there must have been a mistake and nicknamed her *Friedl*, a boy's name. She laughed and accepted the name, and no one was surprised when I joined the long run of boys—six in all. As the seventh child in our family, I received a special honor. When Paul von Beneckendorff und von Hindenburg became the president of Germany, he wanted to encourage families to produce lots of children to build up the population after the great loss of life in World War I. To motivate them, he promised to become the godfather of any child who was the seventh born. That is how I came to have the then-German president as my godfather.

Front two rows, from the left: a friend, Erwin, Manfred, Mama, Edmund, Waldemar (in front of Papa), and Walter. Grandma Koehler stands to the right of and behind Mama. C. 1934

The home where I was born in 1930—apartment 7B, Kasernen Strasse in Sprottau—was marked from the street by one ground-level window in an army of windows looking out from a long and high brick wall. Our window stared across the stone street at the *Kaserne,* the army barracks—a big brick building surrounded by a high, wrought-iron fence. We never saw the inside of that building.

Our apartment had two bedrooms, a big combined kitchen and dining room, a bathroom with running water, and the family room. One bedroom belonged to my parents, the other to the children, and I always shared a bed with one or two of my brothers.

The family room was the center of our home. There we sang together and listened to my mother read the Bible. There I listened to my brother Kurt's stories of the war. There I fought with my brother Manfred, and there my parents whipped us for coming home late. The family room taught me how life works and how I should view God.

In a corner of the family room, a drawing of Christ hung above a small pump organ, one of two pictures on the walls of that room. The picture seemed huge to me. Drawn in pen on white paper, it portrayed Christ's hair falling about His face in scraggly lines and a crown of thorns pressing into His brow, drawing drops of black blood that tainted the blank forehead.

I didn't pity this Man, though the drawing demonstrated His suffering. I didn't feel a great sense of thanks at the sacrifice He made for me. His face scared me. *He* scared me. His eyes were fierce. My brothers and I always minded our behavior when we were in the family room because His eyes pierced into us wherever we went, keeping record of every mistake.

We minded our behavior whenever *anyone* was watching. As good German citizens and Lutheran church members, our parents taught us that if we did good things, we would go to heaven, but if we did bad things, we would go to hell. Our parents and teachers constantly reminded us that every action had a direct consequence. They told us about the love of God, but I thought God loved only good kids, good people. He didn't love the ones who did bad things, and that included me at least half the time.

In my family, it wasn't easy to be good. Papa whipped my older brothers for small things like coming home with muddy pant legs or dirty shoes. By the time my brother Manfred and I came along, Papa must have tired of the discipline battle, for Mama had the responsibility of keeping us in line. She was very nearsighted and refused to wear glasses, so when she looked at us after we did something wrong, her eyes burned into us intensely, both to focus on us and to drill in the seriousness of our actions. We knew she meant it when she looked at us like that. When we did something really bad, she used a whip with a foot-long handle and seven leather straps tied to the end. We never complained about getting whipped, but we did cry when the leather straps hit us.

Sometimes instead of whipping us, Mama made us peel the downy part of feathers off the shaft to make filling for our feather beds and pillows. She was an efficient woman—disciplining us and getting housework done at the same time. She kept a whole pile of feathers, and she tallied up our offenses until we had earned at least an hour's worth of feather peeling—shaft in one pile, down in the other. I found sitting there and keeping my legs still harder to endure than being whipped. You had to be careful not to move too fast, or you would blow half the down you had plucked off the pile and onto the floor. Chicken and goose feathers are tiny to begin with, and my neck and legs ached after an hour of sitting still and pinching millimeters of down between my fingertips.

The feather peeling didn't make my mother stop whipping us, though. The last time she whipped me, I had come home past my curfew at the age of thirteen. Things like coming home with muddy feet, throwing spitballs in class, coming home past curfew—these were bad. They made you bad, and they made God stop loving you.

Some of my actions didn't deserve punishment; some of them did. One time, my friends and I rode our bikes to a traveling amusement park that came to our town twice a year. We thought it would be fun to get away with stealing something from one of the booths, so my friends distracted the attendants while I sneaked to the back of the booth, grabbed a watch, and put it in my pocket. Long after my curfew, my friends and I returned to where we had parked our bikes, and I found that my bike had been stolen. One of my friends let me ride home on the back of his bike. When I got home, Mama was waiting at the front door with her whip in her hand to punish me for breaking curfew. When she found out I had lost my bike, she whipped me more. I didn't dare tell her that I had "won a watch at the fair." She wouldn't have believed me. After a few days of living with a conscience full of guilt, I decided to bury the watch next to an oak tree, where I'm sure it lies still today. That day, I learned that there are consequences to every action.

The idea of good and bad was so warped in my family, though, that we often suffered fear of punishment for innocent actions. Just after I turned nine, my brothers Edmund and Manfred and I went outside to play. At thirteen, Edmund was much bigger than I was, and I didn't dare fight with him as I did with Manfred. When we played, he always bossed us around.

This particular day, he decided to be the cowboy and made us the horses he was training, which meant he chased us around the yard with a whip. "Yah, yah!" he shouted, snapping the whip in the air.

Tired of being prodded, I ran to the tree in our yard and scampered up the trunk to get away from him. Suddenly, I cried out in pain. I had jammed my knee against a broken-off branch and poked a deep hole in it.

I came down the tree with blood running down my leg. Edmund took one look at me, dropped his whip, and ran to get a first-aid kit. Our parents weren't home, so he crouched down and wrapped my knee to stop the bleeding. "Don't tell Mama.

Don't tell Mama," he said as he unrolled the dressing to cover the blood. I wouldn't dare tell Mama. We were always afraid that we'd get punished, even when accidents happened.

Two days later, I started limping. My knee had become infected. Papa noticed and asked what had happened. I started crying and couldn't answer him, but Edmund was there, and he told Papa for me. Papa didn't punish me. I think he figured I had endured enough pain. But Edmund probably got a whipping. Our fear of our parents and, by extension, of God was always stronger than the pain, no matter how much our troubles hurt us.

During most of my childhood, Friedl, Erwin, Kurt, and Walter lived away from home. Friedl went to a boarding school and then, when I was six, got married. The boys worked at apprenticeships. In Germany, after completing eight years of elementary school, children who didn't go on to higher education learned a trade in a three-year apprenticeship. Perhaps because Papa couldn't afford higher education for us, he sent us to find apprenticeships. Erwin became apprenticed to an electrician, Kurt to a dairy specialist, and Walter to a baker. They worked for their masters and received room and board in exchange.

When they all came home for the holidays, we spent the days ice skating and sleigh riding and then crowded into the family room. Erwin picked up the family violin, Kurt played the harmonica, and the rest of us sang. Papa sometimes tried to mumble along, but he was no good at singing, so he sat down at our little pump organ underneath the drawing of Christ. He didn't know how to read music, but Friedl wrote numbers beside the notes for him, so he played by number.

My mother had a beautiful voice, and she always sang something around the house as she dusted and made up the beds. One of her favorite songs was *"Soli Deo Gloria."* When we all got together, she often led us in that song.

> Every thread made on my spindle,
> Every fire I gently kindle,
> Every morning I am greeting,
> Every harvest I am reaping
> All to honor God with fervor,
> Here and there to praise my Savior,
> *Soli deo gloria* [all to the honor of God].

As the youngest and smallest, I always stood in the center of the circle when we gathered at the organ to sing, and I sang as loud as I could, smiling up at my strong big brothers, watching Erwin draw the bow across the strings, hearing my mother's sweet voice strongest of all as she nodded her head to keep time—and always the drawing of Christ peered down at me from above the organ. Even the music and the happiness I felt as we were all together could never completely drown out the message in His eyes.

Perhaps a boy's father has the strongest influence on his view of God. I found many contradictions in my father. Sixty years ago, we certainly didn't communicate with physical affection. I can count on one hand the number of times my *mother* hugged me. But Papa made it clear in other ways that he cared for me. He worked long hours at the office and then did backbreaking work in the garden until after dark to provide food for us. He bought me ice skates when I turned seven. He planned family picnics. Those were his ways of hugging me.

He also showed me how to hunt for invisible treasure. The year I turned eight, he woke me up early on Saturday mornings and took me to the forest to look for mushrooms. It was always a serious mission—I knew we had to find mushrooms so Mama could fry them for dinner that night. Papa was serious about Mama's cooking.

Papa and I walked silently several feet apart. With each step, my feet sank in a little and then bounced up from soil that was made rich and spongy by decaying leaves that had collected over the years. An occasional bird song cut through the trees, a bright sound in the crisp morning air. Each exhaled breath formed a cloud of steam.

I looked out of the corner of my eye at my father's long strides, and I tried to match them, to walk strongly, yet softly. The trees stood, hushed and solemn, around us. My father and I were alone in a great, secret cathedral.

My eyes darted over the ground, eager to find mushrooms and fill Papa's basket. Then he would reach his arm toward me, motioning me to stop. "Go ahead, son—pick them up." I looked to the ground but couldn't see any mushrooms. He came over, bent down right in front of me, and brushed aside a handful of loose topsoil. There they were—four plump mushrooms, each a different size. This happened many times, Papa brushing away the soil and revealing luscious mushrooms where a second before there had been only dirt. Later, I realized he found the mushrooms by watching for places where the ground rose in little mounds, but back then it seemed like pure magic.

Papa required that dinner always be ready on time, and Mama, with her clocklike regimen, never disappointed him. None of us dared to be late. As we entered the kitchen, the stove was directly to our left. Mama usually stood there, frying the food, and my older brothers—once they were too big to be whipped—often pinched a piece of fish off to drop in their mouths as they passed her on their way to the table. Mama made fresh bread and cabbage soup and fried sausage or mushrooms or fish that Papa had just caught.

We usually chattered happily during mealtimes. I remember vividly, though, several terrible scenes. The three or four of us boys were still at the table talking about how to earn some pocket money and Mama had gotten up to scrape the leftovers into a pan on the stove when Papa got up and began to shout. "Therese, I saw him watching you." The way Papa barked her name made me jump.

"I didn't ask him to," Mama said. She stirred the leftover soup absently.

"He has no reason to look at you that way?"

Mama shook her head and shrugged her shoulders.

"You gave him no reason to look at you that way? There can only be one reason he looked at you that way! And I saw you speak to him last week in the street. What do you say to that?"

"I don't remember talking to him."

"You don't remember? Maybe this will help!" and he slapped her across the cheek.

Mama looked up from the pot to Papa, shaking her head quickly. "Albert, I don't remember. I don't remember."

Papa punched her in the ribs. "You *will* remember." He grabbed her by the arms and shook her. "You *will* stay faithful, do you hear me? I am your husband, and you will respect me. Do you understand?" When he took his hands off her arms, I saw white marks that turned red where his fingers had grasped her.

"Albert, no such thing happened. I am——" A punch in the side interrupted her. "Faithful," she finished, beginning to sob.

Another slap on the face.

Mama continued to sob. "I *am* faithful. I *am* faithful. I *am* faithful."

Papa didn't hit her lightly; he really pounded on her. My mother's body—a punching bag.

We had to watch. We couldn't get out because my parents and the stove stood between us and the only exit. So Edmund glared at Papa, Manfred stared out the window, and I, the littlest boy, slid down in my chair till my neck was level with the tabletop. Then I bent my head down and watched through my eyelashes until Papa left the room and Mama stumbled to her bedroom, stifling sobs, too ashamed to look any of us in the eye. I couldn't look away, and I promised myself then that I would never hit a woman.

That was my father: a man who could make mushrooms appear magically in the dirt, who showed me how to fish and gave me ice skates—and a man who whipped his sons for coming home dirty, and, on a whim of jealousy, beat the woman he had sworn to love—beat her until her face was swollen and her arms black and blue. This was my view of a father, earthly and otherwise.

My picture of God was further developed through my school. At the age of six I began attending the Adolf Hitler Schule, which was just two blocks from our apartment. A very modern building for those days, Adolf Hitler Schule was big enough to educate all of Sprottau's children. The school had a huge sports arena, which also held important city meetings, including the ceremony in which I was sworn into Jungvolk.

I loved school. Every morning, we began the day standing in straight lines around the flagpole in the plaza. We raised our right arms above our shoulders in a salute and sang the national anthem, *"Deutschland, Deutschland, Über Alles."**

Deutschland, Deutschland, über alles,
über alles in der Welt,
Wenn es stets zu Schutz und Trutze
brüderlich zusammen hält, . . .

Germany, Germany above all,
above all else in the world,
When it steadfastly holds together,
offensively and defensively,
with brotherhood.
From the Maas to the Memel,
from the Etsch to the [Little] Belt,
Germany, Germany above all,
above all else in the world.

Then, as the flag went up the flagpole, we sang *"Die Fahne Hoch"*†[Raise High the Flag], the Horst Wessel song, the song that had become the anthem of the Nazi Party. A thousand children held their arms high every morning and sang a song named for the faithful follower of Hitler who had been assassinated by his own people and now was held up as a national hero.

---

* *Encyclopaedia Britannica Online,* s.v. "Deutschlandlied," http://www.britannica
.com/EBchecked/topic/159893/Deutschlandlied (accessed May 22, 2009); italics added.

† Allies & AFRICAKORPS North Afrika & MTO Campaign Research Group, "Horst-Wessel-lied ('Horst Wessel Song')," AfrikaKorps.org, http://www.afrikakorps
.org/songsofthedesert.htm (accessed May 22, 2009).

Raise high the flag, close ranks, now all together,
Storm troopers march, with firm and steady tread.
Souls of our comrades shot by Reds and by the enemy
March with us too, and swell the ranks ahead.

Half of us were under ten. Many of us were not yet four feet tall. Yet we shouted out the honor of joining ranks and killing and dying for our country. Every song we sang taught us that our country was more important than our own lives, and that conquering the world was a noble mission worth dying for. Hitler promised that he would usher in the thousand-year kingdom that is prophesied in the book of Revelation. He called it the Third Reich. So, not only were we fighting for our country, we were fighting to usher in Christ's reign on the earth. That meant that we must consider everyone else the enemy. In Germany, bringing about Christ's reign would be done with hate, not love.

Even before the war, the political scene was interwoven with each lesson. As early as the second grade, Herr Schmidt talked about Hitler's philosophy during religion class.

"What do we learn in the New Testament about Jesus' nature, children? We read in 1 Peter 1:19 that we are saved 'with the precious blood of Christ, as of a lamb without blemish and without spot.' What does this mean?" Herr Schmidt looked over his glasses around the room.

"What does it mean to be without blemish and without spot? Let's see. Who can tell me what a lamb looks like?" He waited. All forty of us knew that someone was going to have to answer. Helmut Keller, a dark-haired and usually quiet boy in the front row, raised his hand.

"Yes, Keller. What does a lamb look like?"

The small boy stood. "Lambs are white and woolly and soft, and sometimes they have midnight black noses that are even softer than their wool."

"No!" Herr Schmidt's voice was sharp at first, but he quickly reined it back. "No, Keller. You are right that they are white and woolly and soft, but they never have the blemish of a black nose, and neither did our precious Lord." He raised his eyes to the ceiling. "Pure means white and fair, and, as our Fuehrer teaches us, the whitest, fairest kind of person is the Aryan. What is an Aryan, class?"

Several hands popped up. "A German!"

"Right! So our Lord Jesus Christ was an Aryan German— the superior race we are so privileged to be a part of."

Herr Schmidt drew a painting of Christ from behind his desk, held it up, and turned it from side to side so we all could see it. "We now know He looked something like this," he said.

In this painting, Jesus' hair flowed around His face, but it was blond and smooth, not as scraggly as portrayed on the drawing at home. And Jesus had bright blue eyes. I preferred this picture because His eyes didn't pierce into me like the ones at home. In fact, He didn't seem to care whether I was in the room at all.

CHAPTER THREE

The Revolver

Papa must have sensed that trouble was coming. In December 1938, he moved us from our apartment in Sprottau to a small farm outside of the town. We lived on the bottom floor of a large farmhouse that had been divided into four apartments. My friend Eberhart Paula's family lived upstairs.

Mama cried for weeks about having to care for livestock, pump water from the well, and walk fifty feet through the snow to get to the outhouse. When the war began on September 1, 1939, though, she stopped crying, because the town folks barely scraped by on their rations while we had plenty of milk, meat, and eggs from our goats, pigs, and poultry.

From our little farm, I could see onto the grounds of a military airport where pilots were trained and new planes tested. As the war escalated, the maneuvers in the sky transfixed my friends and me. We knew every model of plane. Every so often one crashed in the fields that surrounded our property. My friends Kurt Leider, Eberhart, and I always ran to the crash site to see what we could salvage before the soldiers arrived. I found many souvenirs, including a revolver and strings of machine-gun ammunition. A soldier showed me how to use a hacksaw to cut the ammunition in half, stuff breadcrumbs in the open end of the shell and use it in my revolver. I was ready to fight the enemy.

There were all kinds of crashes. Some of the planes just belly landed because the landing gear hadn't worked and lay awkwardly on their bottoms. Others nose-dived into the ground and were badly smashed. But the pilots generally survived these accidents.

While I never saw a pilot at a crash site, Eberhart and I did hear of one who died. We went to the graveside service—the first I had ever attended. It was autumn, and leaves coated the ground.

About fifty people gathered at the gravesite. The military ceremony called for stoic men in uniforms to march in formation, with gun salutes and bugling. While the ceremony went on, Eberhart and I shuffled leaves with our feet and ground pebbles into the mud with our toes. We looked up when they put the coffin down into the hole. We watched them lower it slowly, and we heard the soft thump when it reached the bottom.

The pastor began to read 1 Peter 1:3, and the congregation joined in: "Blessed be the God and Father of our Lord Jesus Christ, who according to His abundant mercy has begotten us again to a living hope through the resurrection of Jesus Christ from the dead."

After a pause, the pastor continued the liturgy alone, his voice loud and strong. "Almighty, eternal God, we ask you to please surround this place, where we lay our brother to his rest, with your peace through Jesus our Lord."

"Amen," said the congregation.

"We commit this resting place of our brother to the loving care of God the Father and the Son and the Holy Ghost."

"Amen."

"As it pleased the Almighty God to call our brother out of this life, we lay his body into God's earth, so that he will become dust, from which he was taken."

At this point the pastor took a handful of dirt from the tall, loamy pile beside the grave and threw it onto the coffin. "Earth to earth, ashes to ashes, dust to dust." He threw another handful down. "Earth to earth, ashes to ashes, dust to dust." And again: "Earth to earth, ashes to ashes, dust to dust." Then he motioned to a tall man with dark hair, perhaps the pilot's brother, inviting him to toss a handful of dirt into the grave, the traditional gesture of farewell.

The pilot's wife had stood statue-still through the funeral service. When the coffin was lowered, she had watched from the side, her face and neck pale above her black coat. But when the tall man beside her stepped forward and tossed his handful of dirt down on the coffin, something broke inside her. She lunged forward with a deep sob, the first sound she had made during the whole service. She tried to jump into the grave, but someone caught her, and then her relatives reached out to hold her back.

Alarmed by her outcry, the cemetery workers thought they'd better cover the coffin quickly, and they began shoveling dirt into the grave as fast as they could. The pastor tried to keep up, reading the rest of the liturgy quickly and softly, while the woman's body heaved with deep sobs. She was wailing out a sound I had never heard before, and I watched her white face turn red and become distorted and wet with crying as the barrier of dirt between her and her husband grew. With each sob, her body lunged forward, and then, restrained by hands that clutched her waist and arms, she stood, bent, and shook silently.

At this point, an adult grabbed my shoulder firmly, turned me around, and guided me away from the graveside. I saw that the crowd had begun to disperse too, leaving only the family, the cemetery workers, and the mumbling pastor. I tried to look back, but the hand on my shoulder was pushing me along, and I had to keep my eyes ahead so I wouldn't trip.

Death surrounded me as I grew up: my brothers died when I was in my early teens; every week the pastors announced the death of church members in the war; the radio regularly announced the battlefield death counts of our enemies. But familiar as I was with news about deaths, I'd never seen anything like this funeral. Most of the people in our town hadn't. Usually, we just took death as it came. It was, after all, part of conquering the world. We were taught that those of us who did suffer should never let our cries escape the walls of our homes to tarnish pure German streets with sorrow.

Part of this calm acceptance came from our religion, which said that we should simply accept whatever Providence ordered. But we were also heavily influenced by the propaganda that surrounded us—especially those of us who were children. The leaders of Jungvolk trained us like soldiers. They gave us each a uniform, and we each had a *fahrtenmesser*—which resembled a Swiss Army knife—to wear on our belts. We practiced maneuvers, marching four or five hours away from our homes and sleeping in barns or in camps in the forest. We even trained with guns.

The Adolf Hitler Schule (School)

Some Sundays, we marched in front of the churches accompanied by drums and trumpets and sang Nazi songs—much to the dismay of the people inside. The songs were about the honor of dying for one's country and about the Nazi vision, with lyrics such as "today Germany belongs to us; tomorrow it's the whole world." I loved these maneuvers and felt proud to wear my uniform and march in step with my comrades.

Papa didn't always let me go to these meetings, though. He made the excuse that he needed my help at home on the farm. He didn't join the Nazi Party until 1941, and only then because he would have lost his job with *Finanzamt,* the government's tax collection agency. Regardless of what Papa thought, however, at nine years old I believed the lessons my teachers taught us about our supremacy, and thought I would fight to the death for my country. I looked forward to every opportunity to show my courage and commitment.

When we moved to the farm, I had to leave Adolf Hitler

Schule and attend a two-room school, four grades in each room. Once the war began, we weren't allowed to ride our bikes to school; the authorities didn't want us to squander rubber needed for the war effort by wearing out the tires. So at ten years of age, Eberhart and I walked a mile and a half to school and back every day. Teachers, though, could ride their bikes to school.

Every morning before entering the classroom, we sang the national anthem and "Die Fahne Hoch" as the flag was raised. The dew sparkled on the grass, the white light of early morning glinted off the flagpole, and I felt proud of the beautiful country I lived in. I stood with my chest puffed out, head held high, eyes straight ahead, ready for Frau Hofmann to give the signal to salute.

One morning, Frau Hofmann rode up behind me as I walked to school alone. (Eberhart must have been late or sick that day.) I turned when I heard the crunch of the bike tires on the gravel and smiled when I saw it was my teacher. "*Guten Morgen* [Good morning], Frau Hofmann!" I said. She glared at me, pedaled faster, and sped past without a word. I put my hand to my head to smooth my cowlick, wondering if my appearance was offensive in some way.

At the flagpole, I stood at attention, waiting for the command to sing, but there was only a long silence. Then Frau Hofmann called my name: "Leonhardt!"

I turned my head to look at her.

"You will not participate this morning," she said. "Step out of formation."

I stood outside the circle while my fifty-some schoolmates raised their arms and sang to the flag. When their voices were silent, she didn't dismiss us to the classrooms as usual. Instead, she barked my name again: "Leonhardt!" She pointed her finger toward the ground next to her and held it there until I stood at her side.

"Students, Leonhardt greeted me with *'Guten Morgen'* this morning. I would like to make an example of what the Fuehrer thinks of citizens who don't honor him with every word." She slapped me on one cheek and then the other.

"Leonhardt, I will tolerate only 'Heil Hitler' from now on. Do you understand?"

I nodded, keeping my chin high.

"If the fatherland is truly in your heart, this will come from your lips. Only traitors forget to honor their leader with every word."

She swiveled about and marched toward the classroom door. "Come, students," she said. "We have work to do."

No one spoke to me as they walked to the school building, and I didn't move until even the last first grader had filed past me with wide eyes.

Blind obedience was constantly drilled into our heads, and it worked. One afternoon when Eberhart and I were about twelve, we were at home alone—our mothers must have been in town on errands. We knew Hitler was going to address the country that afternoon, and Eberhart's family had a radio, so we went into his family room, turned the radio on, and waited, cross-legged on the floor. Before Hitler spoke, the national anthem was played. By the time the third note rang out, Eberhart and I were on our feet. With our right arms in the air, we sang the entire song. *"Deutschland, Deutschland, über alles, / Über alles in der Welt . . ."* Just the two of us were in the room, but we didn't think twice about standing and saluting and singing our hearts out.

The brainwashing we received in Jungvolk was strong enough to make us salute in an empty room, and it was strong enough to make me believe Germany couldn't lose the war. Our Fuehrer had promised the wonder weapon, and it was only a matter of time before we would destroy all our enemies. When the war finally did end, it took me four years to admit we had lost. I kept thinking, *Something's going to happen; something's going to happen.*

Even our games echoed the destruction we were raised to value. In addition to chasing plane crashes, Kurt Leider, Eberhart, and I loved to play cowboys and Indians, inspired by translations of James Fenimore Cooper's books. We made bows, arrows, and spears from the branches of willow trees, and we fought battles against a group of boys from another housing complex.

An old farmer had a piece of land right behind Kurt Leider's home with a tool shed on it filled with plows and other farming implements. The shed served as our goal when we played cowboys and Indians and other war games. A windbreak of trees and bushes about three hundred feet long stood near the shed. We usually made our camp there, and the other kids stationed themselves in the woods on the other side of the shed. The first gang to make it through the arrows and spears and to occupy the tool shed won the game. If the shed was locked, as it usually was, we had to crawl in through the window before we could call ourselves the winners.

The war games seemed innocent enough at first. Then one day Kurt and I crouched behind two trees in our camp, shooting arrows over the shed to the enemy's camp as fast as we could reload our bows. Suddenly, I heard a plunk on the ground behind me just as I let an arrow fly. Turning around, I saw a foot-long section of a thick branch with a rope hanging out the end. The rope was burning.

Puzzled about what the odd missile was, I just stared at it. But Kurt scrambled over to it, grabbed it, and threw it as hard as he could back over the tool shed. *Boom!* We saw a flash and heard a loud bang as the branch exploded in the air. The other gang had made a hand grenade by cutting a section of a branch in half lengthwise, hollowing it out, filling it with gunpowder, and running a fuse through the middle.

The war game ended for that day. Maybe we realized momentarily how badly we could have hurt each other.

Our schoolteachers taught us that, as members of the superior race, we didn't have to respect anyone weaker than us, which meant we could terrorize anyone who didn't have the strength or authority to make us respect them. At times Kurt and I stole pastries from the bakery. And when it was dark, we hid behind bushes and threw sticks at the wheels of passing bicycles. If one of the riders fell, we sneaked away to a place where we could laugh until our stomachs hurt. Our victims never knew where the sticks came from.

Our teachers also taught us that the elderly didn't deserve our respect—that their physical weakness made them flawed. So Kurt and I found an old man to torment, the man who owned the tool shed. Soldiers took him away to a concentration camp for part of the war, and his two daughters had to do all the farm work during that time. I don't know why the authorities took him, but when he came back, he was very grumpy, which made him even more fun to tease.

Kurt had a canoe, and on one occasion we paddled upstream

to the riverbank behind the old man's house, bringing our handguns with us. Night had fallen by the time we got there, and we shot our guns in the air until the cylinders were empty, hoping to scare the grumpy old man. Then, we floated silently back downstream and beached the canoe at Kurt's house—two special-operations soldiers with another mission accomplished.

Most of what we did was just boyish mischief, but our pranks did reflect our dreams. Every boy dreams of becoming a strong man who does great things. Our society taught us that honoring and supporting our leader and stamping out those weaker than us would make us into men like that.

Among my heroes were the men I read about in *Robinson Crusoe* and *The Last of the Mohicans*. But I dreamed most about becoming a pilot. The summer I turned twelve, I often went out into a field near the airport in the late afternoon, after I had brought the slop home from town for the pigs and before Mama called us for supper. I lay down in the tall grass, picked a long, golden stem to chew on and watched the planes fly over. At times, a couple would dance across the blue expanse, their engines' sounding a distant putter-roar. Sometimes, a glider plane would appear soundlessly, using the air currents to stay aloft. With each plane that passed, I imagined myself with goggles on, a control stick in my hand, and a revolver on my belt. I wanted to be in the sky, above the clouds—to be a pilot, not just a copilot.

Under the shadow of the war, our household shrank: my father was drafted in 1943 and Manfred in 1944, so only Mama and I remained to run the house. A teenager now, I substituted a passion for running for my mischievous games. I got up before breakfast every morning and jogged to build up my speed and endurance, and when I got home, I doused my head in cold well water because Mama said that would increase the circulation of my blood.

I continued in Hitler Jugend. In the winter, the local branch sponsored a two-week ski trip during which a disabled officer of the *Waffen-SS* (the combat arm of the Nazi Party) instructed us in skiing. One night during that trip, my friends and I started goofing around after curfew. The officer, who had lost an eye and an arm in the war, soon stood in our doorway and ordered us outside in our nightgowns. (Pajamas were not yet in fashion.) For the next couple hours, he drilled us on the ski slopes in the dark until we performed flawlessly. From then on, we didn't make a sound after curfew!

My brother Kurt had been sent from the Russian front to a nearby military hospital. Though his leg and foot were wounded, he managed to limp home to visit us almost every day. Always the entertainer, he told great stories of the winter he had spent in Russia. When the temperature dropped to forty degrees Fahrenheit below zero, the soldiers' guns became so cold that they wouldn't shoot unless the soldiers warmed them up—and the only way they could do this was to urinate on them! Kurt captivated me and terrified Mama with the story of the night when the Russians invaded his camp. The only weapons they carried were their knives so they wouldn't make a sound. Kurt was on guard duty that night, and he said his deep tan saved him, because it enabled him to blend into the shadows of the trees. The bright white faces of his comrades reflected the moonlight, making them obvious targets.

As 1944 came to a close, most of the adults around us had

lost hope of victory. We didn't have a radio, but we could see the signs that our forces were in retreat. For months, German families driven out of the East by the invading Russians moved past our house on foot, or, if they were lucky, by horse and wagon.

Every night, immigrants knocked on our door—weary, frozen, and begging for shelter. Mama never turned anyone away. They piled on the living-room floor and into the barn. Mama always kept a pot of stew on the stove. By this time, even on the farm, she had to ration food, so dinner was always thin vegetable soup, coffee substitute, and, if we were lucky, a bit of bread or sausage. Mama used the same "coffee" grounds for days—by the time she replaced them, our drinks were just hot water with the faintest hint of bitterness.

The refugees weren't the only ones on the move. Many soldiers saw that the war was lost. No longer driven to fight, they abandoned ranks and traveled west, trying to blend in with the refugees. The Waffen-SS made periodic checks of the immigrants, and when they found a deserter, they shot him. Soon, they decided the renegades weren't worth a bullet, so they hung them on the telephone poles lining our streets. Before long, there was a soldier in uniform hanging from every telephone pole on my street for as far as I could see. Their bodies, frozen solid by the blizzards that blew through our town, formed a monument to Hitler's philosophy: fight to the last man, and if the last man stops fighting, kill him.

Even dead bodies hanging along the street become commonplace when you pass them every day on the way to school. I still believed we would win the war, that Germany was worth fighting for, that Hitler was bringing a magic weapon. I kept my revolver at my side, ready to fight to stop the Russians.

One evening in December, when the sun had been down for hours and our guests had already finished their bowls of soup, we heard a heavy knock on the door. Mama opened it with me right behind her, and there stood a soldier holding a bicycle, his hands purple from the cold.

"Do you have room for me?" he asked and coughed from deep in his lungs.

Mama looked at him, her mouth pursed in a straight line. She knew what would happen if she was found harboring a deserter. But then she opened the door with a nod. As he came into the house, I saw that pieces of his uniform were torn out where there should have been insignia patches. I watched him sip his soup down. Soldiers fascinated me.

In the morning, I knocked on Eberhart's door while the soldier ate breakfast. When the soldier was ready to leave, we were outside, waiting for him.

I tapped on his arm. "May I show you something?"

He grunted and nodded.

I grinned, puffed out my chest, and held up my revolver, expecting him to inspect it with an experienced eye and recognize me as one of his comrades.

He looked at the gun, scanned me up and down, up and down, and then looked straight into my eyes and, using a term I won't repeat here, called me a despicable fool. He shook his head slightly, his eyes never leaving mine, and said it again. His words were firm and full of calm hate. Then he walked his bicycle into the nearby field, where he turned and rode west on the farm roads between fields, away from the main roads. For him the war was over. There was no more use for weapons.

For me, the war was just beginning, and I longed to prove I was a man.

On February 12, 1945, two months before I would have graduated from eighth grade, the German army began setting up artillery on the east side of town, just beyond our farm. Only a trickle of immigrants straggled by our house that night. The next day, we heard explosions from the airport—the German army was blowing up the planes they couldn't move west and didn't want the enemy to use. Stories were whispered from neighbor to neighbor about entire families committing suicide rather than allowing themselves to fall into the hands of the Russians. Stories we heard said that the Russians were torturing all the men and raping women or girls in their path.

When I woke up on the thirteenth, Mama was packing clothes and pots in a bundle. She packed, unpacked, and repacked all day, and when I went to bed, she was still packing. I fell asleep to the sound of airplanes exploding on the tarmac.

CHAPTER FOUR

Frozen in Escape

On February 14, the sound of pounding on the front door
woke me out of a heavy sleep, my heart thumping. I opened my
eyes. It was still dark. Then I heard rapping on the window
next to the door and muffled shouting: "A train is leaving at
eight o'clock this morning. Anyone who wants to leave should
leave." *Rattle, rattle, rattle.* "The train will leave at eight o'clock.
Be there if you want to get out!" The noise of the pounding
diminished as the person carrying the news rattled the windows of our neighbors' apartment.

By the time I pulled my pants on and stumbled into the living room, Mama was closing the door she had opened to hear
the neighbor's message. I looked at the clock. 5:00 A.M. We
had three hours to get to the train station.

Mama had stayed up all night, and she was ready to leave.
She had put the most important belongings into packs that the
two of us could carry: lots of warm clothes, some smoked pork,
a cooking pot, birth certificates and family trees, pictures from
Friedl's wedding, the letters announcing Walter and Erwin's
deaths, and more warm clothes. The two big bundles stood

Elfriede and Siegfried's wedding, December 1937 (Waldemar, left, and Edmund and Manfred, right, first row. Kurt and Erwin, near center, second row. Mama, Oma, and Papa on Siegfried's left.)

next to the door. They looked lonely.

As Mama closed the door, she turned to me. "You'd better get dressed, Waldemar," she said. "We should leave as soon as possible to make sure we get on the train. Put on several layers of clothes so you'll have some to change into. There isn't room in the packs for all the clothes we'll need. I'll make some coffee while you get dressed."

I donned several pairs of socks and two pairs of pants and stuffed my revolver into the back of my pants. I wanted to have it handy.

I ran downstairs, stood next to the table, and slurped my coffee. Mama had made it stronger than usual this morning. She sat very quietly at the table, turning her head frequently to stare at the kitchen and the living room. Her eyes were red from lack of sleep. When I wasn't looking at her, I could feel her studying my face. Finally, she brushed some strands of hair from her face and said, "We'd better go."

I handed my coffee mug to her, and she rinsed it in the bucket we washed dishes in. I was still very hungry and thought of the canned juices and fruit in the basement that we wouldn't be able to take with us. Mama had saved them for special occasions, and when we did eat them, she gave us each very small servings to make them last longer. The strawberries were my favorite. Whenever I asked her for more, she scolded me for taking too much. But this morning I thought I'd give it a try. "Mama, could I have some strawberries?" I said.

She looked up at me with tears in her eyes. "Eat all you want," she said in a voice just above a whisper.

I ran down to the basement, grabbed a quart jar, and ate the whole thing right there. The flavor of summer burst on my tongue, filled my mouth, and slid down my throat. When I had eaten all the berries, I drank the juice and licked every last drop from the mouth of the jar.

I climbed the stairs, smiling at the sweetness, and saw that Mama had her coat on and one of the packs on her back. I pulled on my overcoat and scarf and picked up my pack, finding it heavier than I expected. "Why do we need so much stuff, anyway?" I asked Mama.

She didn't answer. She just opened the door and said, "Let's go." I glanced quizzically at her as I passed her in the doorway. I thought we'd be gone only for a week or so.

When we were out in the dark, I looked back at the apartment house and saw that all the lights were out except for those in the Knappes' apartment, which was next to ours. Eberhart's family and the family next to them were already gone.

Mama stepped over to the Knappes' kitchen door and rapped on it. Herr Knappe opened the door. He was in his mid-eighties.

"Aren't you coming to the station?" Mama asked.

"No," Herr Knappe said. "We're staying."

Frau Knappe stuck her head out under Herr Knappe's arm and said, "We'll take care of the animals." She nodded her head and tried to look cheery, but there was a quaver in her voice.

Mama paused as though she wanted to say something else, but then she just shook their hands and said, "*Gott segne Sie* [God bless you]."

As we walked away, I looked back at the Knappes' kitchen window. I saw Herr and Frau Knappe sit down at the table, and I noticed that their friend, Herr Dunkel, was there with them. "They must think they're too old," Mama said.

As we rounded the corner and headed toward town, I looked back to see the light shining from the Knappes' kitchen window out onto the snow and the outline of the four chimneys of our house black against the starlit sky. Little did I know I wouldn't see my home again for forty-eight years.

We walked the two and a half miles to the train station with the heavy packs on our backs. As we neared the station, the eastern horizon began to hint at sunrise, and we heard the first blasts of the new day's fighting. The Russian line east and north of Sprottau was pressing hard on our soldiers, and as trees and fences and buildings began to appear in the blue of dawn, the short blasts of artillery fire grew into a continuous rolling, roaring sound.

When we arrived at the train station, there were soldiers from the home front waiting outside to make sure every able-bodied man stayed to fight. As Mama and I stood in line, waiting to get through the station door, a soldier approached me and put his hand on my shoulder. "This isn't the time for a faithful citizen to leave, young man," he said. "Stay here and protect your home. Fight for the fatherland. The Fuehrer needs you."

I felt my revolver burning against my hip under my coat. This was my chance. I nodded and began to take a step forward to ask the man where to report for duty. Then a hand grabbed my shoulder, and suddenly Mama was between the soldier and me. "You stay with me. You are the last one," she said. She steered me back in line. She stared at the soldier and said it again: "You stay with me." He turned away, but her eyes stayed fixed on him until we shuffled through the station door. It seemed that they were burning a message into the back of his head: *You will not take the last one.* She kept her grip firm on me until we got on the train.

Although we had gotten to the station early, the train was already full of people. But they stuffed us in, and many people after us. When the train finally moaned out a whistle and lurched from the station, early morning sun fell through the windows and lighted on suitcases and hat-covered heads. The people in the passenger car were quiet. I heard only hushed exchanges between mothers and children and the occasional wail of a small child. Those of us who hadn't found seats stood with anxious, tired minds and listened to the thunder of the artillery, which even the clacking of the wheels on the rails beneath us couldn't drown out.

When the train stopped at Guben, a town northwest of Sprottau, Mama shook my arm and said, "Let's get off here and catch the connection to Goerlitz. We'll go to Friedl's." I grabbed my pack, and we pushed through the crush of people to the door. We waited several hours in the station for the connection and arrived at Friedl's house in the evening.

My sister's husband, Siegfried, was in the air force, fighting on the eastern front, so Friedl took care of their four young children by herself. My *oma* [grandma] Koehler had evacuated to my sister's house a week earlier, so Mama's and my arrival made eight of us in the tiny house.

Five days after we arrived in Goerlitz, orders came through: all elderly citizens and families with young children were to evacuate—the Russian army had advanced close to Goerlitz.

My oma was seventy-eight years old, and Friedl's four children were all under the age of eight, so we had to leave. We piled the packs Mama and I had brought on a handcart and added some food, clothing, and documents that belonged to my sister's family. Before we left, I buried my revolver in Friedl's backyard so it would be safe until we came back. Again, I thought I would return within a week. Then the eight of us set off for the train depot.

At fourteen, I was the only man in the group. Since there were four children and four adults, each adult took a child. Friedl and Mama carried the two youngest kids, Oma Koehler held five-year-old Anita's hand, and I was in charge of seven-year-old Dieter. I had him help me pull the cart.

The buildings near the depot were closer together than those at the edge of town, and the streets were smoother, made of flat, broad granite. We moved slowly as evacuees from all over the city joined together in a sluggish mass. Suddenly, the air raid sirens began to sound their alarm, and, just like a storm that is directly overhead, the lightning and thunder of the attack assailed our eyes and ears simultaneously. Within a second of the first wail of the siren, Russian planes screamed in the blue sky above us. Fighter planes, they dropped small bombs and shot at everything that moved.

I let go of the handles of the cart, and we all ran into the hallway of the nearest house—dust and debris flying in with us—and huddled as far inside as we could get. The whistle of the bombs and stutter of the guns shook the air around us, and we could hear the shrapnel and bullets colliding with wood, metal, and flesh outside of our shelter.

With each blast in the street, more pieces of wood and rock and clouds of dust flew in the front door of the house, which still stood open. We stared at it for a few seconds with our hearts pounding, and then my sister yelled, "Somebody needs to close the door!"

Out of the corner of my eye, I could see Friedl. Her free hand was on Anita, she was cradling the baby with her other arm, and Dieter and Anita clung to her skirts. Oma Koehler and Mama were huddled together with little Peter, their eyes closed. I felt cold, hard stone against my back and palms. I knew Friedl wanted me to close that door, but I couldn't move. I just stood against the wall and shook.

Nobody else moved either. Finally, Friedl pried the kids loose, jumped forward, and closed the door.

We heard a few more blasts, which were dampened by the thick door, and then, as quickly as it had started, the attack was over and all was silent.

As the adrenaline subsided and I could feel my limbs again, I felt guilt pulse through my body and tighten in my chest. Here I was, the only man in the group, supposed to protect my family, and I hadn't been able to move. When we finally inched our way onto the street, I followed my sister with my head down.

Our cart lay on its side, broken, and our belongings were scattered all over the street and sidewalk. We gathered everything we could carry and made our way to the train station.

Once inside the station, we went downstairs to the hallway, where we could register to get on the train for refugees. As we got in line, we heard a large explosion from somewhere above us. All of us turned our heads and tensed, ready to run for shelter if needed. I thought for a second that the Russian planes were back. It was completely silent for a moment, as though the entire train station was on pause, but we heard no aircraft. Then a man screamed, and his scream was followed by a chorus of other screams, wails, and yells—sounds I'd never heard before.

I took seven-year-old Dieter's hand and said, "Let's see what's happening." We left the others in line and ran through the main concourse to the front doors. People were scurrying about, and others were standing stone still and staring outside.

My first glimpse at what was outside stopped me dead in my tracks. It's still as clear in my head as a photograph. In front of the entrance to the depot, body parts lay scattered on the granite blocks that made up the plaza. These were not just bodies that had been damaged. Here was a headless torso cut off at the knees, half-covered by what was left of a green wool coat. Over there was the back of a head of thick hair matted with blood. I saw bits of grey, green, and blue cloth mingled with the red and white of torn flesh. Not one head was connected to shoulders.

I noticed a hand and forearm with a bit of torn grey cloth still clinging to it, and I realized that just moments before, that arm had pulsed with life. It had stretched back to pull a coat on, had held a mug of coffee to lips. To human lips.

I looked up. The whole corner of the building across the street was rubble—an avalanche of bricks and mortar and stone. A bomb had exploded inside, and the explosion had blasted into the street, destroying everything up to the station doors. In the middle of the plaza was the island at which street-cars stopped. It was demolished. A streetcar had been standing there when the bomb exploded; the side facing the train station had been blown out, the metal was now frozen in the form that the blast given it. In the door of the streetcar hung a torn body, like a piece of meat hanging in a butcher shop. It was the closest thing to a whole body in all the wreckage—a gruesome witness to the carnage.

I stood silent. I knew that if my family had arrived at the train station four minutes later, the parts of my body would have been scattered across that plaza too.

The scene burned into my memory, and I felt something die within me. This was real. Here, the war soaked through my skin; no effort was required to grasp it. This was it—the way the world was.

I felt no compassion or sorrow for the casualties. In fact, I felt nothing, not even weariness—nothing but a coldness that permeated my whole body. When my heart went cold, I just turned and led Dieter back to the family. We had to catch a train. And I became a body that moved with a heart that was frozen.

CHAPTER FIVE

Hunger

The explosion in the train plaza made me understand the chaos of the war for the first time. And as we made our journey toward safety, it was clear that the entire world was in chaos. All the people I saw were suffering from a lack of security as well as of physical necessities. For me, as a fourteen-year-old refugee, there was no better evidence of this hunger for fulfillment of every kind than the emptiness of my stomach.

At fourteen, most boys can out eat their fathers, and their mothers complain that they can't keep the cupboards full. Once we left Sprottau, my growing body hardly ever got enough food. I spent the next four years thinking of nothing but food and Hitler's wonder weapon. My dreams of being a pilot were buried as deeply as my ability to feel emotions, and this time of physical hunger marked the beginning of a lifetime of hunger for other things—mostly for love and meaning.

The train we caught at Goerlitz turned out to be a freight train. Soldiers loaded us into cattle cars, which left us nowhere to rest but on the grimy floor. We huddled together there, unable to avoid touching the other families packed in around us.

We traveled like that for a day, going south forty-five miles to Reichenberg (now Liberec in the Czech Republic). At Reichenberg, we transferred to a passenger train, which was much more comfortable though still overcrowded. The aisles and all available floor space was packed with the bags and other belongings of the passengers. But Mama, Oma, and Friedl were able to find seats that faced each other, which made caring for the children much easier.

On board, I befriended a couple of other boys my age. We met three girls, and the six of us piled in the back of the passenger car, on top of the bags and suitcases. And for the next five days, we slept sitting up.

We traveled to Prague, in the Czech Republic, and from there, west to Bavaria, in southern Germany. Our train stopped frequently on side tracks to let military trains pass. The officials warned us that there might be air raids, and on one occasion they stopped the train and we had to run and hide in the nearby woods until enemy planes had passed.

I was hungry the whole time. The smoked pork Mama had brought lasted only the first day, and we stopped only once a day at soup kitchens the Red Cross had set up at train stations. The meal was always the same: cabbage soup with one piece of bread. Those who were last in line got the thickest part of the soup, but no bread. I never got full.

In the middle of this hunger and chaos, my new friends and I talked and tickled and flirted just like normal teenagers. We sang Hitler Jugend songs to pass the time, and one boy played on a jaw harp, making what sounded like a cat's meow.

When the train stopped for food, my friends and I ran out into the crisp winter air to get in line as fast as we could, jostling our way through a crowd that smelled of five days of body odor. We slurped down our soup and then trudged back to the train, where we climbed on top of the luggage again and shifted around, trying to get comfortable. I didn't think much about my family at this time, only about surviving and having as good a time as possible.

On the fifth day, we stopped for the first time in Bavaria, and the locals fed us a feast of hard rolls and milk. It was January 25, only eleven days since we had left Sprottau, but it seemed like years had passed. From then on we stopped at every little station along the tracks. Farmers with horse-drawn wagons waited to take the people who got off the train to safe lodging.

Our turn to debark came at Karpfham. Sleighs and wagons were lined up there, ready to be loaded. A farmer with a leathery face nodded to us and helped my sister lift the children into his sleigh. He drove us nine miles over chewed-up snow and mud to Sankt Salvator. The road took us through a tall forest, up and down many hills, and then through fields covered with great frozen dirt clods that lay waiting for the ground to thaw so wheat and barley and oats could sprout once again. Even when we were riding through fields, the edge of the forest was always in view. We didn't talk at all in the several hours it took us to reach the town. We were all tired, dirty, and hungry, and I just wanted a full meal and a warm bed.

The citizens of Sankt Salvator were well organized. They already knew where each of us would stay. Friedl and her children went to a farm about half a mile outside of town. Mama and Oma were taken to a room in town. And a young boy led me to a house on the edge of town, where the forest began. It had been dark for several hours by the time we arrived at the house.

A woman with dark hair opened the door and looked at me with wide eyes. Then she rattled off something in the Bavarian dialect, which I couldn't understand. The boy replied to her, and she said something else. She didn't look happy.

I looked at the boy and he told me her complaint. "Frau Mayer says she signed up to take a girl. That's why she's confused. But she'll let you stay until the problem is straightened out."

I nodded my head in thanks and followed her into the house, where she led me to a small room upstairs with a balcony. When I was standing in the dark outside the house with a week's worth of beard, an overcoat down to my ankles, and a scarf wrapped around my head, I probably had looked much older than fourteen and even rougher than I felt. No wonder she was uncomfortable! But she took another look at me in the lamplight of the room and must have seen that I was really just a scruffy little boy, because she smiled kindly before closing the door behind me.

When Frau Mayer called me down in the morning for a breakfast of bread and milk, she told me she had decided to keep me. She and her fourteen-year-old daughter, Annie, could use my help since her husband was away fighting in the war. I began to help by milking their cow, drawing water from the well, and collecting firewood.

When I first arrived, I went to school with Annie. But they soon closed the school because most of the teachers had to go into the service, so I never officially finished elementary school. After that, I had all day to help with the chores and wander the town thinking about my growling stomach.

Although Frau Mayer shared everything they ate with me, I never got full. After a meal at the Mayers' house, I often walked to Mama and Oma's house, and Mama shared with me what little they had to eat. Since she didn't have any fat or oil, she fried potatoes in water and coffee substitute that she had already used several times. From there, I walked to see my sister. The farmer's wife had fallen in love with Friedl's children and always shared some extra food with her, so Friedl always had something for me to eat, though the servings were small. I often took Dieter to the forest, pulling a little hand wagon that we filled with dry sticks and twigs for Friedl's woodstove.

Frau Mayer made bread sometimes, but there seldom was enough to fill us up. So she often sent me to the bakery to buy bread with our ration cards. To get any bread, I had to arrive before the sun was up and stand in line, stamping my feet and blowing my breath into my collar in an effort to keep warm. Sometimes, when I reached the counter, everything had been sold out, and I had to go home empty-handed. At times the bakers said they were sold out even when they weren't because they were saving some bread for their friends. We were outsiders, so we always came last.

Most townspeople didn't like us. Often, when I was standing ahead of a townsperson in line or just walking on the streets in town, I heard them call me and other refugees *saupreussen*— "pigs from Prussia." It didn't really matter where we were from. We weren't natives of Bavaria, so we were saupreussen. They always made sure they said it loud enough for us to hear.

Two weeks after we arrived in Sankt Salvator, I made my daily visit to the farm where Friedl lived. Like most refugee families, she and her four children lived in one small, crowded room. As she handed me a mug of coffee and a piece of bread, she said, "Waldemar, I need to go back to Goerlitz. The children are getting bigger, and when we left, I had room for only one extra set of clothes for each of them. Besides, Peter kicks in his sleep, and with all his kicking and my having to get up to nurse Christina, I've been getting only a couple hours of sleep every night. I need to move Peter out of my bed. We haven't really had all the blankets we need since we got here anyway, and I have so many clothes and blankets at home. Will you go with me?"

While my sister was talking I noticed her face. She was only thirty-one years old, but the bags under her eyes showed that the months of caring for four children without her husband were starting to wear on her. I agreed to go, and Mama offered to babysit while we were traveling.

At that time in the war, civilians were allowed to travel by train only thirty miles in one stretch, or to the nearest station beyond that distance. It was 350 miles to Goerlitz, so we decided to travel in installments, buying new tickets at each stop.

Our journey started early in the morning with an hour's walk to the train station at Ortenburg. From there, we rode the train eight miles north to Vilshofen and another thirty to Straubing. As soon as the train stopped there, I jumped off to buy two more tickets to the next station. The line at the ticket counter was longer than I expected, and before I knew it, the train with my sister, my coat, and my identification papers pulled away. I was left standing in the bustling station with only enough money to get back home or on to the next station.

I stayed in line and began dreaming up stories about why I wasn't on the train with my sister. When I reached the ticket master, I mumbled that someone had stolen my ID papers and my ticket when I got off the train to stretch my legs and that my sister had left without me. I'm pretty sure he knew I was lying, but he seemed to feel sorry for me anyway, and he got me on a train that went directly to Weiden, which would be my sister's next stop after Regensburg.

Somehow, my train was delayed, and when I arrived at Weiden, my sister's train had already left. Now I was farther away from home and didn't have enough money to return there. I used the rest of my money to buy a ticket thirty miles north to Eger, which is now called Cheb and is in the Czech Republic.

By then, I had been traveling two days and was weak from hunger and lack of sleep—and two hundred miles still lay between me and Goerlitz. However, I didn't have the time or energy to be scared. At the Eger station, I noticed a Red Cross office and offered to volunteer in exchange for some food. They agreed, and for a couple of hours I helped dish up food for the refugees. In return, they fed me, offered me a cot to sleep on for a few hours, and gave me a ticket for the rest of the journey to Goerlitz. All this time, Friedl had no idea where I was, and I didn't know whether she was still in Goerlitz. We didn't have telephones with which to stay in touch.

When I walked through the door of Friedl's house in Goerlitz, she had packed everything she needed and was just about to leave. She ran to me and cried and hugged me close and stroked my hair. I felt my heart swell with relief and joy at being with her again—the strongest emotions I had felt since the bomb had exploded near the train station. Focused on surviving loss, hunger, and constant attacks, we were caught off guard by the blessing of being reunited.

We spent that night in her house to get a good rest. The next morning I dug up my revolver, and we left. The Russian army took Goerlitz the following day. Since we were considered refugees again, we didn't have the thirty-mile limit, and we arrived in Sankt Salvator that same day. It had been only four days since we left, but it felt like an eternity. I was just one of thousands of people lost, hungry, and confused as trains crisscrossed Germany, a country in retreat. When you are continually hungry and confused, these feelings become a dull ache you hardly notice, but they hang like weights from your shoulders everywhere you go.

The war raged on, and soon the fighting roared through Bavaria. We heard reports of American planes bombing the larger cities around us and scanning the forest, searching for a German army installation that was hidden there.

On Sundays during this time, I changed into clean clothes and walked with my family to the nearest Lutheran church, which was in Ortenburg, an hour away. Often, American bombers surprised us, and we dived into the ditches, clean clothes and all, until they flew on. Those Sundays, we arrived at church late and dirty.

One day, as I walked home from Mama and Oma's house, a plane suddenly rose above the trees right in front of me, strafing the dirt road with its machine guns. It was so low to the ground that I could see the pilot's face, life-sized, and the leather cap on his head. I dived behind a big oak tree just before bullets raised little geysers of dust right where I had been standing. There was a fence overgrown with ivy in front of the tree, and looking through it, I saw the pilot's face as he passed barely twenty-five feet away from me—the first enemy I had seen. He looked mean. He was out to kill.

Several other planes whizzed by after him, also strafing the ground. I heard the drone of their engines and the sound of their guns fade for a moment, and then they got louder again. The second time they flew over, they didn't follow the road. Instead, they came from all directions, each strafing a different street through town with their machine guns. They passed over three more times.

Among the displaced people in Sankt Salvator was a Hungarian army group, refugees who were no longer fighting but who still wore their uniforms. I think that may be why the Americans attacked our village—they saw those uniforms. One of these soldiers had been walking along the road and jumped behind the oak tree with me when the planes surprised us. As the planes flew over a second time, each from a different direction, this soldier lost his mind. He ran circles around the tree, first one way and then the other each time a plane buzzed overhead.

When he began acting that way, I thought, *They're going to see him. They'll start shooting at us!* I quickly scooted into the ditch by the fence and lay flat to the ground with one eye watching the crazy man yelling and running in circles with his hands in the air. I didn't feel anything myself. I wasn't scared. I just accepted the airplanes, machine guns, and bombs as part of life. I had known that first pilot would have shot me if he had seen me, so I had gotten out of the way. And I knew that if I had a gun, I would have shot him. That's all I knew. I had left my shaky knees in Goerlitz along with my ability to feel fear or sadness or happiness.

After several passes with their machine guns blazing, the planes dropped some small bombs in the center of the village. I was about a hundred yards from the village center, and I felt the explosions shake the air. Then I heard the airplanes roar away, fade to a dull hum in the distance, and then leave a breathless silence. The whole attack hadn't lasted longer than fifteen minutes.

The crazy soldier stopped running and dropped his hands to his sides, but it took a while before anyone else in our village moved. I listened carefully for any sign of an engine, and then I stood up, brushed off my knees, and walked back to Oma and Mama's house. By that time the townspeople were beginning to peer out of their doors and assess the damage, women and children still clinging to each other. A bomb had hit the building next door to Oma and Mama, but by the next day we carried on as if nothing had happened. What else could we do?

Each day, I spent my time learning the Bavarian dialect, walking to visit my family, and helping Frau Mayer with chores. The raw cold of winter thawed into the fresh wetness of spring, the frozen clods in the fields crumbled into loamy mud, and I thought about food. I still assumed that Hitler would win the war—that he would use the wonder weapon he had promised and defeat our enemies. But from day to day my main concern was trying to fill my growling stomach. Like a CD player stuck on repeat, my mind never got past the thought of food.

Then it was May 7, 1945. Hitler had committed suicide. And now, in Rheims, France, five hundred miles from where we were, General Alfred Jodl placed his signature on a piece of paper that called for the unconditional surrender of the German army. So, on May 8, I woke up in a world without war, a war that had been the backdrop to my childhood and early teen years. I still believed Hitler's wonder weapon would make us victors.

Several days later, American soldiers came to Sankt Salvator and sent messengers to each household with orders to turn in all weapons. While Frau Mayer emptied her kitchen drawers and filled a bag with all her silverware and cutlery, I buried my handgun near a tree behind her house. Then I took the bag with her silverware to the town center and stood in line. When my turn came, I handed the bag to an American soldier. He looked inside and then handed it back to me with a grin, nodding that I could keep it all. Frau Mayer was overjoyed.

Since the war was over, Mama had more energy with which to worry about me, and she focused on my hunger. She talked to farmers in the area and found that Herr Haselreiter, who ran the Hanerl Farm, which was next to the farm where Friedl lived, would take me on as a farmhand. In exchange for my work, he gave me room, board, and twenty reichsmarks a month—at the time, the equivalent of about five U.S. dollars. I slept above the pigs' barn on a mattress-size linen bag filled with straw.

Herr Haselreiter's oldest son, Martl, was my age, and we became great friends. He taught me everything he knew about farming. We arose at five o'clock in the morning in the spring and at four o'clock in the summer. Before breakfast every morning, we cut fresh grass with a scythe to feed the horses and cattle. We then cleaned and brushed the bull, five cows, and five horses. After breakfast, we worked in the fields. It was hard work, but life was better than it had been in the winter months. I had lots of food to fill my stomach, and I also had Martl's friendship.

A few of the farm's 140 acres were still forested, and some of the rest of the acreage was pasture for the livestock to run on, but the majority of the land consisted of fields of rye, wheat, barley, and oats, which all had to be harvested by hand with a scythe. Men did the scything, and a woman gleaned behind each man, picking up the grain he had cut and wrapping it in small bundles. Herr Haselreiter hired extra help during the harvest. Sometimes Martl and I worked at scything and some-times at gathering and bundling the stalks of grain. Whatever job we had, we tried to do it faster than anyone else.

When it was time to harvest the hay, Martl's father sent us out to help an older man named Franz. We were to scoop the hay with pitchforks and toss it as high up on a horse-drawn wagon as we could reach. Martl and I were supposed to harvest one row and Franz took the other row, with the wagon be-tween us. Franz also had to drive the team when it was time to move forward, so Martl and I were sure we could beat him to the end of the row.

Before long, Franz moved ahead of us, and we shouted to each other, "Go! Go! We have to beat him!" We moved our scrawny, fourteen-year-old arms as fast as we could. Soon mine started to ache with every toss of the pitchfork. I watched Franz out of the corner of my eye. He moved so smoothly—now coaxing the horses forward, now tossing hay to the top of the pile. He seemed to be moving slower than we were, but he just kind of floated down the row, while Martl and I were all sweat and pitchforks sticking in the ground.

"Go! Go! Go!" we yelled, but we never did catch up with him. He laughed at us, and we laughed, too, at our inability to keep up, and our laughter made us go even slower. That, in turn, made us laugh so hard that our stomachs ached.

Besides entertaining ourselves during our work, Martl and I managed to get into some mischief with girls as well. During the war, schools in big cities like Berlin had evacuated their girls' dormitories to rural areas, where the girls were scattered among farms to be kept safe. One school sent their students to our neighborhood, and we liked to flirt with the girls, even though they were a couple years older than us.

One evening, Martl and I decided to try out an old Bavarian tradition called *fensterln*. When a young man is in love with a young woman whom he's been forbidden to see, he sneaks a ladder to her bedroom window and knocks till she opens. Many stories and songs feature such love affairs.

Always curious to see what we could get away with, Martl and I picked a Berliner named Else Byrd. We didn't really want to go fensterln seriously—we just wanted to knock on Else's window and say Hello. So, when everyone else had gone to sleep, I put a ladder up to Martl's bedroom window, he climbed down, and we walked the fifteen minutes to the farm where Else lived, carrying the ladder between us. Just as we leaned it up against the side of the house, the yard lights came on, and we heard yelling and swearing. One of the servants had caught us. He didn't tell anyone, but he spoiled our fun. Several escapades like this got us into trouble, but they didn't stop us for long. The entertainment was worth the risk!

On Sundays, I still walked to Ortenburg with my family to go to the Lutheran church. Lutheran boys go through confirmation classes at the age of fourteen so they can take the sacraments, and Mama was determined that I would get those classes even in Bavaria, where the majority of people were Catholic.

I can't remember the name of the pastor at Ortenburg, but I can still see his face. He was in his late forties and had a full head of hair. Every Sunday this pastor's preaching captured and held the congregation's attention. My mother loved him, and I loved him too.

As he led us through the fundamental church beliefs and the Bible, he took the time to explain their meaning to us. In his confirmation classes I felt religious conviction for the first time in my life. Mama was happy that my heart was being touched.

When that pastor spoke, I felt a certain awe about God. I realized the immensity of His power, and I respected it. However, I also received the impression that if I did something bad, I couldn't escape the consequences, and I came to believe that I had already lost my chance at being saved—a conviction that I kept to myself.

A few days before the service at which I was to be confirmed, my pastor was seriously injured in a car accident. Another pastor confirmed our class in the formal service, but our pastor wanted us to visit him on his deathbed so he could give us his blessing too.

Mama went with me to the room along with the other boys and their mothers or fathers. Our pastor wore his black robe as always, but his voice was weak, and each movement seemed to be a painful struggle. Yet he was determined to bless us. I watched him place his hand on the shoulder of each boy who knelt by his bed and bless him with a Bible verse—a different Bible verse for each one.

As my turn approached, a lump came to my throat. Even at the threshold of death, this man wanted to share his strength with me. When I knelt by his bed, I glanced up into his eyes. They had a look unlike that of any other eyes I had seen. They weren't sharp and condemning like those in the picture of Christ in my old living room. Nor were they absent and disinterested like those of the Nazi Christ and like the eyes of so many men during the war. Instead, they rested upon me with care and told me it mattered to him that I was there, that his last breaths were well spent on me.

I bent my head.

"Waldemar"—the formerly powerful preacher had to force each word out of his mouth and sometimes had to stop for a breath in the middle of a sentence—"the verse I have for you . . . is in the Gospel of Saint John, chapter six, verses sixty-five through sixty-nine. . . . This is it: 'And He said, "Therefore I have said to you . . . that no one can come to Me . . . unless it has been granted to him . . . by My Father."

" 'From that time many of His disciples went back . . . and walked with Him no more. . . . Then Jesus said to the twelve, . . . "Do you also want to go away?" ' "

My pastor paused to catch his breath.

" 'But Simon Peter answered Him, . . . "Lord, to whom shall we go? . . . You have the words of eternal life. . . . Also we have come to believe . . . and know that You are the Christ, . . . the Son of the living God." ' "

My pastor took a moment to swallow before lifting his hand to my shoulder. "God bless you, my son."

I looked into his eyes and nodded silently.

Our pastor died within the week, but I have carried his blessing with me all my life: "We have come to believe and know that You are the Christ, the Son of the *living* God."

Little did I know then that my physical hunger as a refugee was the first in a long line of hungers, and that my pastor's blessing held the key to the fulfillment I would not find for decades.

CHAPTER SIX

The Violin

One day during harvest in July 1945, Martl and I ran into the dining area just a little late for *mittagessen,* the big noon meal. The rest of the family and hired help were sitting at the table and waiting for us, so I slid quickly onto the bench and Martl slid in after me. Then Herr Haselreiter bowed his head and mumbled a prayer, and Frau Haselreiter uncovered a steaming bowl in the center of the table.

Frau Haselreiter had made dumplings again. Usually, they were just made of flour and water, but we were lucky that day—she had added bacon bits to them. The bowl with the dumplings also had chunks of meat in it, and we all took our two-pronged forks and eagerly speared the food to get it onto our plates.

I was starving from a full morning of work, and as I jabbed at a dumpling in the bowl, I missed and splashed a little of the liquid it was sitting in onto the table. Martl, who was always joking around, elbowed me in the ribs. "Ha! I've never told you the story of the priest who came for mittagessen last year and tried to jab one of Mama's dumplings, have I?" I shook my head and smiled, even though I had heard the story a hundred times. He went on. "The dumpling was so hard that his fork just slipped off the side. The dumpling shot out through the open window, and . . . Papa, you tell him what we found when we went back to work."

Herr Haselreiter cleared his throat and pushed a bite of dumpling into his cheek. "Our rooster lying dead, with Mama's dumpling next to his head. He never knew what hit 'im!"

Martl's father laughed a toothless laugh and pounded on the table, looking out of the corner of his eye toward Frau Haselreiter. She sighed and scowled with a slight twinkle in her eye. "You lie. Don't believe a word of it, Waldemar. They tell untruths."

Martl watched his mother mischievously and poked a dumpling over and over with a fork, saying, "Clunk, clunk, clunk," until she swatted at his arm with her hand. "Enough! Enough!" she said. "Eat already, or I'll feed your share to your brother!" Martl didn't want to take any chances, so he shoveled his dumplings onto his plate.

I scooped some milk out of one of the pots on the table with my spoon and slurped it down. There were no cups, just a pot of milk for every two people. I never wasted time talking as long as there was still food to be eaten—especially in the middle of the day when we still had lots of work to do.

Then, Martl's sister Maral pointed out the window. "Look. Someone's here!"

We all turned to look toward the gate in the yard and saw my sister Friedl and her children were coming through it.

That's odd, I thought. *They never come to visit in the middle of the day.*

Mama and Oma appeared next. That was even stranger.

They had to have walked all the way from town. Then behind them came another person and— "My father!" I yelled and jumped over Martl and the table, spilling milk and knocking Martl's dumplings off his plate. I ran out the door and was across the courtyard before the Haselreiters knew what had happened.

I threw myself into Papa's arms, and we hugged tight, the only hug I ever remember him giving me. "My boy," he said and wouldn't let me go. Neither of us wanted to let go.

When we finally stopped hugging, we pulled back and looked into each other's faces. Then we turned, and, with my father's hand on my back, walked to where the Haselreiters were waiting to be introduced. When Papa had left two years before, I had to look up to see his face. Now, we stood shoulder to shoulder as we walked across the courtyard.

Papa had been stationed in Denmark, and although we had written many letters to him from Bavaria, he had received only one. But that letter contained enough information for him to find us. As soon as the allied occupiers released him, he came straight to us.

The Haselreiters and Papa shook hands, and for a while there was much jabbering between Frau Haselreiter and Mama and between Martl's sisters and Friedl. Herr Haselreiter watched for a few minutes and then said, "It's about time we get back to the fields. But Waldemar, you go ahead and take the rest of the day off." He paused and then said with a wink, "I probably wouldn't get much good work out of you anyway!"

We spent the rest of the day asking Papa questions and telling him about our adventures since we had left Sprottau. We said that it was actually a blessing in disguise that he had been drafted when he was because if he had stayed home, they wouldn't have let him evacuate with us when the Russian army invaded our town. He would have had to stay and fight with the *Volksturm,* the homefront army, and that would have meant certain death.

Papa had fought in World War I, so when he was drafted in the Second World War, it was as an *unteroffizier*—similar to a sergeant in the U.S. Army. After he was drafted, he went first to Poland and then to France with his troops. There, they asked for volunteers to join the occupational forces in Denmark. He raised his hand because he had grown up in Prussia and spoke a Low German dialect similar to Danish.

Papa spent the rest of the war in Denmark in charge of troops that had the job of doing recovery on the crash sites of planes that were shot down. When the plane-crash site was in the countryside, he and his troop stayed with the farmers who lived in the area. Since he did the translating for all the other Germans, he became good friends with some of the Danes.

After we had shared the basic details of what we had been doing since we last saw each other, he opened the sack he had been carrying with him. "I have more goodies back in Oma and Mama's room; this is all I could carry with me here," he said and handed me a jar. "Waldemar, here are strawberries for you. And Therese"—here he pulled out a parcel—"Havarti cheese. Barba Spelman sent that especially for you. You would like her, Therese. You are like each other."

Papa had a little something for all the family—things we hadn't seen for years. When he finished handing out the gifts, he turned to Mama. "Therese, let's go to Denmark. I've already picked out a bride for Waldemar. She's a beautiful girl. Good

Lutheran girl. Tabitha. She is the Spelmans' oldest daughter."

He glanced at me and raised his eyebrows. "Beautiful girl, Waldemar." Then he turned back to Mama. "What do you say, Therese?"

Her face was stoic. "No."

"You would love Denmark."

"I'm not going."

And that was that. But Papa loved Denmark.

After the German surrender, the allied occupiers released members of the German army slowly. Papa was lucky. Many soldiers wandered through the country looking for their families without any idea where they were or even if they were still alive. Mama often stopped these drifting groups of soldiers and asked if they had seen my brothers Edmund and Manfred; we hadn't heard news of them since we fled Sprottau. But no one she met had seen them.

Our hopes rose when the Red Cross set up a database for all displaced refugees and released soldiers. We thought maybe now we would be able to find my brothers. But again, we never heard from them. Edmund and Manfred had disappeared into the ocean of missing people. We eventually came to believe they had died. That, however, was very different from getting the news that they had died. Papa's return had given us great hope for their survival; then that hope lessened over the years until there was none left, only a dull ache—the sense that something was missing but we couldn't put our finger on exactly what.

Kurt and his wife, Wally, joined us soon after Papa did, and so our family was restored as much as it ever would be. My parents had begun the war with seven children. Now, it was down to Friedl, Kurt, and me. I think Papa's finding all his children either dead or grown up softened him. He was much more sentimental, and I never saw him strike or yell at my mother again.

Papa soon got a job as a security guard at a church in Sankt Salvator that had collected goods for displaced families. There were new and old clothes and toys and a mishmash of other goods. Papa stood several watches every week to make sure no one stole the goods, which the congregation gave to displaced persons but only to those who asked for them. He also got some clothes for us. I wore what I received for years.

As soon as Papa had found a job for himself, he took on the task of finding an apprenticeship for me. Since the war was still raging at the time when I should have graduated from eighth grade, I hadn't followed the normal process of becoming an apprentice. Instead of sending me out on my own as he had my brothers, Papa traveled with me from town to town, looking for an opportunity for me to become an electrician so I could fulfill my dream of following my brother Erwin's career path. Although several master electricians were willing to take me in, they couldn't provide me room and board in the lean post-war days. Finally, I decided I would settle for any trade—for any master who would offer me room and board. The proprietor of the Geiger Bakery in Vilshofen agreed to take me in, and I bade farewell to my friends, the Haselreiters.

When I had worked at the bakery for five weeks, however, we learned that the labor department had ruled that businesses could employ only residents of their county because of the large number of refugees looking for work. This made me jobless once again. So, Papa and I went to the seat of our county, hoping that some other opportunity would turn up.

A farmer outside Sankt Salvator hired me to work for him while I waited for an apprenticeship. I had worked a whole year on the Hanerl farm, so I had the strength and the skill to do just about any job he assigned to me.

In August, two weeks before I turned sixteen, we finally got good news: a baker in *Ering am Inn*—Ering on the Inn River— needed an apprentice. Papa and I traveled the twenty miles by train for the interview, and master baker Rudolf Forstner hired me on the spot. Papa signed over my guardianship, and my childhood was officially ended. I would spend the next three years working like a slave at *Baeckerei Forstner* (Forstner Bakery).

Herr Forstner and I produced all the bread and rolls, his wife tended the shop, and a girl my age, Ursula, kept house. I had thought that farm work was difficult; now I learned the true meaning of exhaustion. Every weekday, Herr Forstner and I began work at 3:00 A.M., and we started making the bread for Saturday at ten o'clock Friday night. Every day we worked from ten to fourteen hours.

In exchange for my work, the Forstners gave me a little room with a bed, closet, small table, and chair; all the food I could eat; and two marks—the equivalent of fifty cents—a week. In the second year they raised my pay to the equivalent of $1.25 a week, and $1.75 a week the third year.

That first year I managed to go home almost every weekend. After I cleaned the production area on Saturday, I grabbed my bag of laundry and took the train to Karpfham. When I arrived there, I walked nine miles through the forest to Sankt Salvator, which took me three hours. About the time I could see the lights of Sankt Salvator, Mama and Papa usually met me, and Papa carried my bag of laundry for me, which during the long walk had come to feel like it weighed twenty pounds. On Sunday, I slept in late, ate mittagessen with my parents, grabbed my clean clothes, and made it back to the bakery by the evening to set the sour and sponge for Monday's production.

I hated working at the bakery. It was hard physical labor and very boring for my restless young mind, which longed to learn about the great thoughts of the world, not knead dough all day. I wanted to quit many times. I had never wanted to be a baker. So, for the first time in my life, I started to pray on my own, asking God to help me get through the hard days.

Then I met another displaced person from Silesia, Herr Ehrenberg, who had been the director of a school of music. He offered to give me piano lessons in exchange for some bread and rolls Frau Forstner gave him to supplement his food rations. I loved it. I practiced during my naptime, never less than an hour a day. When Herr Ehrenberg moved away, I found another displaced person to teach me, a Russian woman who wore black-rimmed glasses, always dressed in black, combed her black hair back in a bun, and who ran her fingers furiously over the piano keys.

A year after I began playing the piano, I met Dominik, the son of a Bohemian displaced person. His father made violins, and both he and his father played for me. Then they let me pick up a violin. I touched the bow to the strings and scratched out a few squeaky notes. There was something about the motion across the strings and the sound of the violin that inspired me to keep trying, and after a few visits, Dominik's father had me producing solid notes. I couldn't stay away from their home and ran over to pick up the violin every chance I got.

When I told my parents of my new interest, Papa bought me

a violin from a craftsman for fifty marks. I got permission from Herr Forstner to take violin lessons, and soon stopped taking piano so I could focus more energy on the violin. When Dominik's family moved away, I heard of a Hungarian displaced person who had taught in a school of music and played in the Budapest Symphony Orchestra. He lived in *Simbach am Inn,* so I bought a train ticket to go there once a week and used the rest of my salary to pay for the lesson. In addition to giving me exercises for the violin, he assigned me lots of music theory to study. After work each day, I practiced three or four hours until 9:00 P.M., when everyone else in the house went to sleep and I had to stop. After that, I stayed up at my desk writing notes about theory. Often I was up until midnight, falling asleep then on my papers.

I burned with the desire to learn. In German, it is called *wissensdurst*—the thirst for knowledge. I had always loved classical music, and Bach, Mozart, and Beethoven were legends—giants of men whose mere names I admired. The idea of playing notes they set down on paper excited me. When I started practicing and playing, I realized there is no end to music. You can always learn more, play better, explore new fields. That was just what my curious young mind hungered for.

Before long, Frau Forstner would stop some evenings and stand in the doorway to listen. And Ursula, the young housemaid, leaned on my windowsill as I pulled the bow across the strings. Every exercise I played sang deep into my soul, warming it in a way I had not felt since I saw the aftermath of the bomb in the train plaza.

It was also while I was in Ering that I met Fritz Sir. His father was a well-to-do banker in Upper Bavaria, but because of his affiliation with the Nazi Party, all his possessions were confiscated when the war ended, and he had to work as a construction worker. Fritz, who was my age, and his family lived in a one-room house. He and I had a lot in common. Both of us were homeless and displaced. We shared a love for music. He played the piano and organ, and we both loved to sing. We spent many Sunday afternoons together, entertaining his parents with music, walking the bluffs above Ering, and strolling the banks of the river with his dachshund Waldy running behind us.

One Saturday after Fritz and I had been friends for several months, his parents surprised us by buying us tickets to go to Passau to see Beethoven's *Fidelio,* the story of a faithful wife who risked her life to save her husband from prison. I had never been to the opera before, and Fritz and I didn't say a word to each other during the entire performance—we just let the orchestral music and the voices wash over us. As we made our way to the youth hostel after the performance, we couldn't stop talking about the opera—which arias were our favorite, which parts of the story were most suspenseful.

The next morning, we heard that the entire opera cast was singing Beethoven's *Missa Solemnis* for church at the *Passauer Dom,* so we made our way there. Once again, I was spellbound as I sat on a wooden pew below the cathedral's ceiling and gazed up at the great white columns that led to Renaissance carvings, bas-reliefs of cherubs, and paintings of angels around the throne of God. The voices of the choir and the strings of the violins vibrated through the space all the way to the ceiling and sent shivers up my spine. I imagined that heaven would be like that.

It took me until I was eighteen to notice that Ursula, the housemaid, was a very attractive nineteen-year-old. We started flirting and teasing each other around the house. At first it was harmless, but it didn't stay that way. We started sneaking away for longer periods of time, always careful that our master didn't see us.

Someone must have seen us kissing, though, because one morning when Herr Forstner and I were standing at the workbench rolling out buns, he asked me if I wanted to marry Ursula. I grinned and said, "No!" Before I could take another breath, he slapped me in the face so hard that I fell back. He was a head taller than me and had hands the size of dinner plates.

I took a step toward the door, debating whether I should run away, but Herr Forstner went back to rolling his dough. Speaking very calmly, he said, "I didn't hit you because of Ursula, but because you sneered at me." After that, I knew I would leave the bakery as soon as I could.

In October of 1949, I passed the test for journeyman, which meant I was a qualified baker in my own right. The Forstners laid me off several months later since my journeyman status required them to pay me a higher wage.

Instead of looking for another bakery position, I moved in with my parents to work in a small enterprise—we sold cleaning supplies door-to-door. That meant that we had to peddle boxes of supplies on our bicycles up and down the hilly country of lower Bavaria—very hard physical labor, especially when the dirt roads were muddy from rain or covered with snow in the winter.

At first, we lived with my brother Kurt and his wife, Wally, in their farmhouse, where I had to set up the cot I slept on every night in my parents' room and take it down every morning so we had room to walk around. Soon, my parents and I moved into an apartment in Ortenburg. There we still lived in one room, with me sleeping on a couch at the foot of their bed.

During this time, I continued my violin lessons and kept up my practicing, traveling the thirty miles to Simbach every week to see my teacher. During this time, I took Bach as my role model, remembering the story of how he walked the almost three hundred miles from Arnstadt to Lubeck to learn from the great organist Buxtehude. I believed it was worth making sacrifices to play the music I loved.

While peddling wares, Mama became acquainted with people displaced from German settlements in Yugoslavia. These people belonged to the Pentecostal Church, and Mama asked me to go with her to some of their meetings. We soon became convinced that our baptisms as infants in the Lutheran church weren't biblical, so we both were baptized in a lake in the Bavarian forest.

The pastor had a daughter named Else who had very long beautiful hair because that group of Pentecostals didn't believe in cutting their hair. Else worked in Munich as a housemaid. She was outgoing with a good sense of humor and was very committed to her religion. I started spending more and more time with her. During the week, I worked hard making money and spent all my free time writing letters to her, and before long, I was making the 120-mile trip to see her almost every weekend. We socialized with other couples, and when we were alone, we talked about the Bible and prayed together.

My mother invited Else to come to our home for a weekend. She made her a special meal, and as we sat around the table and laughed, Else seemed to be a part of the family. Her parents

approved of the match, and by 1952, we were practically en-
gaged.

Else and my music gave me a sense of fulfillment from something besides filling my stomach—the first time I'd felt such
fulfillment since we left Sprottau. The pieces of my post-war
life were finally fitting snugly into place.

CHAPTER SEVEN

Stuck in Reverse

In October of 1953, I had many things going for me. I had just given my life to God by choosing to be baptized. A beautiful Christian girl wanted to marry me, and I spent time praying and reading the Bible with her. I played the violin constantly and even got to perform in an orchestra periodically. My life was full of all the good things that hadn't seemed possible when the war ended.

As I thought about marrying Else, I realized that neither the salary of a salesman nor that of a baker would support a family, so I looked for a higher-paying job. I found a position with Deutsche Asphalt in Munich, which allowed me to move closer to Else.

The first Monday of November, I arrived at work right on time. But the crew I was assigned to work with had already left, so I was sent with a truck driver to pick up a trailer-load of coal. When the coal was piled high in the trailer, the driver said he would back the truck up to the trailer. I was to connect the trailer to the truck by lifting the trailer's tongue and setting it down on the truck's hitch when it was directly below the tongue.

It was a brisk morning, cold enough for it to snow if there had been any clouds in the sky. I blew into my gloves and stamped my feet while the driver climbed up to his seat, started the engine, and began to back the truck toward the trailer. Unfortunately, the trailer was parked on a slope and its wheels weren't blocked, so when I lifted the tongue, the trailer lurched toward the truck, which was still backing up. I tried to drop the tongue on the hitch at the right time, but the trailer was rolling so fast that I missed the connection. I dropped the tongue as I had been told to do, and the trailer stopped. But the truck kept backing up, with me stuck in between it and the trailer. I yelled, but the driver couldn't hear me over the noise of the truck's engine, so he kept backing. The truck and trailer weren't perfectly aligned, so the corners on one side came together first—with me between them. Metal pressed into my ribs, and I literally watched myself being crushed. "Help me!" I yelled. "Help!" And then the fear inside me pushed up through my vocal cords in a blood-curdling scream.

Crick. Pop. Crack. My ribs snapped one by one.

I saw some people run out of the nearby office building, waving their hands at the driver, who still didn't hear my screaming. He finally stopped, though, and then pulled forward, and I crumpled to the ground face first and passed out. If the driver had backed up three more inches, my head would have been crushed.

When I came to, a crowd stood around me. Someone held my face off the ground, but they didn't move me otherwise until the ambulance arrived. They feared that I had a spinal injury. When the paramedics lifted me onto the stretcher, I felt an agonizing pain worse than any I've felt before or since.

At the Catholic hospital, a very jolly monk technician x-rayed my whole body, bending me in every direction on his table and cracking jokes. The pain was excruciating every time I breathed or laughed or moved. "Please, stop joking," I gasped, but he didn't listen.

The x-rays revealed that my collarbone had been broken and then pushed together so hard that the two broken ends overlapped an inch, the outer one jutting upward. Almost all of my ribs were broken, and some were so close to my lungs that the doctors didn't do anything for several days for fear of puncturing my lungs. Eventually, they put me in a compression wrap, which they said would help to keep my body in position so I could heal properly.

I spent five weeks in the hospital. Else and other friends from church came to visit me often, but I was always glad when they left because talking hurt so much. When the hospital discharged me, Else's employer made room for me in his home. I stayed there for almost three weeks and then found a room for rent in a woman's home. Her daughter, a young war widow, and the daughter's two girls lived in the home with her.

Two months passed before I was finally able to take care of myself adequately again, and only just before that did the pain I felt when I tried to lift my elbows higher than my shoulders become bearable.

The day before I left Else's employer's house, I spent the afternoon packing my things, putting them in a neat pile in the middle of my room so I could move quickly the next day. Less than an hour before sunset, the sun streamed golden onto the wooden floor from the window on an unusually clear day for January. Still packing, I lifted a jacket and saw my violin case.

For months I hadn't had the energy to think of it; only a few days before I had finally felt the itch to pluck the strings, but somehow, I had never been alone long enough to venture to its place under the pile. Now, Else's employer and his wife were away visiting family for the afternoon, and Else was working in a far corner of the house, clanking pots as she started dinner. All the other rooms around me were silent.

I clicked open the clasps on the case, swung it open, ran my fingers over the red velvet of the lining, and then grazed the smooth, shiny wood of the instrument's body before grasping the neck and lifting it, so light, to my chin. I clasped the violin with my chin, my neck a little stiff, while I used both hands to tighten the bow and smooth it with rosin. Then I cradled the neck in my hand once again and raised the violin until it was fully horizontal and extended past my shoulder.

I winced a bit with the effort, but the pain was so much less than it had been for months that I managed to hold the violin steady at first. I listened for a moment to make sure Else was still in the kitchen and heard the faint, distant rasping of a sponge on metal. Then I touched the bow to the E string. It squeaked a bit as I drew a long note down to the bow's tip.

I decided to play one of the simple exercises I used to play from Louis Spohr—a simple, quick chromatic piece to warm up my rusty fingers. But as I lowered my finger onto the string, I knew something was wrong. Before the accident, I performed this exercise as naturally as I walked. Now, I had to think hard to find the note that should come next. It was as if my fingers and brain had lost their connection.

I struggled for several minutes, trying to let my fingers re-member. But they couldn't. I started to sweat. The part of me that only an experienced musician can understand, the unconscious part that lets the music and notes flow between one's fingers and the strings, was broken.

My arms started to ache from the effort, my collarbone and ribs began to shoot pain through my body, and I couldn't hold the violin anymore. I swung it into the case just as I heard footsteps in the hallway. In a sweat, I clicked the clasps shut as fast as I could and shoved the case under a nearby coat, my eyes stinging, my forehead wet, my hope dampened by those few squeaky notes.

I tried to bring my violin out several more times in the next few months, but that first attempt had made it clear that I had lost it—the ability of my arms and fingers and brain to work quickly together had been crushed between the truck and the trailer. I knew that never again would I feel the vibration from the hollow body singing against my shoulder, singing from my fingertips. As work filled my life after my recovery, I lost the will to keep trying to play the violin, and I also lost the passion, beauty, and drive music had given my life for six years.

When I moved into my rented room, I tried going back to work at Deutsche Asphalt, but the work was too hard for my still-healing body. Then, a friend of Else's employer found a job for me in the testing laboratory of Krauss-Maffei, a machinery manufacturer with a factory of more than five thousand employees. During the war, they built half-track armored vehicles for the German army. Now, they had switched to building buses, steam and electric engines, and other industrial equipment.

The friend who had found me the job was a senior vice-president in the company, and he suggested that I take night classes from the company to lay a strong foundation for my career. I took his advice, and things looked hopeful. I had a good woman who wanted to spend her life with me, and my vice-president friend even hinted that he had a position for me as a company representative in Spain if I excelled in my classes.

But then several things happened. Working in the laboratory with lots of chemicals, I got an infection in my mouth that gave me a high fever and almost caused me to lose all my teeth. The infection caused my mouth to smell so bad that even Else stayed several feet away from me when she came to visit. When I went to church with Else's Pentecostal friends in Munich, I got the impression that they thought my sickness was a punishment from God, maybe because I hadn't married Else yet. I couldn't make sense of that idea. Everyone else did things that were wrong; why would God punish only me?

I stopped going to those friends' weekday meetings and, soon after, their church services too. Whenever Else asked why I wouldn't go with her, I told her I had to study for my classes, that I had to advance my place in the company so we could have a good life. But I closed up my books as soon as she and her friends left for church. I stopped praying and studying with her and lost interest in religious things altogether. Then we didn't have much to talk about anymore. Soon she quit her job in Munich and moved home with her parents, telling me as I helped her to the bus station that she hoped distance would "make the heart grow fonder." However, instead of my heart growing fonder, I stopped thinking about Else all together. She really deserved better. She was like the rest of her family: simple, diligent, and honest, and I regret now that I hurt her.

On Friday nights, as soon as I got my paycheck, I went home, changed my clothes, and took the bus or rode my motorcycle into town. I walked into a nightclub, sat down at the bar, and ordered beer after beer. I didn't know how to dance, so I just listened to the music and watched the girls dance.

In Germany, one can share a booth with strangers. So after a couple of beers, I would look around and find an empty seat at a table, where I would introduce myself, brag about how much I could drink, and share some laughs until morning. It doesn't matter that your companions are strangers if you're all drunk anyway. All night long we talked and told tall tales and sang along to the music that left our ears ringing. On one such night, someone offered me a cigarette, and before long, I started bringing my own, inhaling the smoke and blowing it out to mingle with the darkness of the room.

My letters to Else were short and distracted, and even from a distance she could tell that my heart had changed drastically. A couple months after she went home to live with her parents, we officially broke off our engagement.

Earlier, I had found my work interesting; I enjoyed the challenge of learning chemical formulas. But without the goal of providing for a wife, I lost interest in my job. When plastics first came out, the engineers of the company I was working for brought a new machine to test in the lab, a machine that made plastic sheets almost as thin as the plastic wrap used in kitchens. On the first day that we began running this machine, the sheets didn't come out right. The engineer blamed me for the problem, so I quit. With just a few words, I threw away the two years I had spent working hard toward a career. I now see that when I stopped seeking Christ, my life started to fall apart. I lost Else and my promising career prospects.

After I quit, I didn't have any passion to motivate me or any desire to do anything toward building a life for myself. Instead, I started running around with women, and I didn't wait for the weekends to go out drinking anymore.

One day I went to a *volksfest*—a state fair—in Dachau, north of Munich, the town where the concentration camp was. When I arrived at the volksfest, I didn't know anyone, so I started chatting with another guy my age, and we set out to cause some mischief. We walked into one of the tents where there was a long table with twenty people on each bench, all of them with beer mugs in their hands. We ordered a large plate of fried chicken and sat down at the table across from two girls about our age.

Rosemarie, one of the girls, had dark hair and eyes that were almost black enough to match her hair. As we all picked at the chicken and drank and told stories around the table, she and I kept making eye contact. At the end of the evening, she gave me the address of the gypsy bar where she worked, and I often went to visit her. She was a cook who specialized in Hungarian goulash. I always let myself in through the back door of the kitchen, sat down at a table in the tiny break room in the back, and waited for when she had a break. Between orders, she came out, sat down, and flirted with me. We talked about our lives, about social events in the city, and about the customers that came through. It was very innocent. We simply enjoyed each other's company.

Not all my relationships with girls were innocent, though. The evenings at the club that I liked best were those in which I could get a beautiful girl to laugh, let me slip my hand around her waist, and lead her away into the night. I was always a one-woman man, so once I met a girl I liked, I went with her for a while. But then I usually ended up backing myself into a corner by telling a bunch of lies that she unmasked and then having to run away. I lived very much upon my urges, doing just what I felt like doing. Looking back, I see that my lifestyle was a way of drowning myself—drowning the gnawing feeling that my life didn't mean anything.

After several months of this lifestyle, I started to notice the woman who lived next door to me—my landlady's daughter. She, too, was named Else. She was twelve years older than me, and had two girls of her own. Her husband had died in the war. This Else wasn't religious at all. She was very cute with a great sense of humor—the typical outspoken Bavarian with lots of spunk. A guy couldn't help liking her.

Since I was her mother's tenant and much younger than she was, Else didn't want her family to know about our affair, so we waited to spend time together until the girls were asleep and her mother had gone to bed. Then we would to go off by ourselves and talk and kiss. We carried on our secret affair for quite a few months.

In the meantime, I got a temporary job selling book club memberships door to door. Then I had surgery to cut off the protruding bone of my broken clavicle, and when I was recovered, I found a job as a baker that paid me room and board and a small salary. If I could have predicted the future, I would have known that in two years the economy in Germany would explode, and a baker's income would double. But I couldn't predict the future. I knew my current pay at the bakery could never support a family, and my failures in relationships with women nagged at me. Bored and disillusioned with life, I thought, *Why don't I go to South America?* Among my classes at

Krauss-Maffei, I had taken a year of Spanish and could speak it pretty well. Going to South America sounded like a great adventure.

I found out that the Lutheran Refugee Service (LRS) helped Lutheran refugees from Silesia find placements in other countries. When I contacted them, they said there wasn't much future for a baker in South America—what about the United States? That sounded like as good a place as any, so I applied to immigrate. The LRS found me a position at the Rockford Home Bakery in Rockford, Minnesota, and I agreed to take it.

When I had a set date to leave, I wrote a letter to my parents in Ortenburg, telling them of my plans. Then I went to visit them for a few days. My parents, Friedl, Kurt, and their families all gathered to say Goodbye. They didn't try to talk me out of immigrating—I had made my decision. They were busy with their families, and I wanted to find my own life.

I remember a conversation I had with Mama and Friedl during that visit. Friedl's husband, Siegfried, had left for the war a very strict Lutheran and came back from a Russian prison a Seventh-day Adventist, after debating with a fellow prisoner who was an Adventist. I had never heard of the denomination and called it an extremist sect because they kept Saturday as their Sabbath and didn't believe in eating pork. Friedl became an Adventist several months after Siegfried returned, convinced that his new beliefs were true. That particular afternoon, I sat at the kitchen table working on my English workbook while Mama and Friedl prepared dinner and discussed their different churches. They talked about the importance of keeping Christ in one's life and debated which Christian principles were the most important. After a few minutes they turned to me. "Waldemar, what do you think?" Mama asked me. "Which of our Christian principles do you think are the most important?"

I looked into Friedl's face, then Mama's, and back again. They both had their hands on their hips, wanting me to join in their discussion. I don't know what got into me, but I replied with a shrug, "I couldn't get anywhere with God, so I'm going to try it without Him."

They didn't say anything in return, but as I shut my book and pushed the chair back to leave the room, I looked at their faces one more time and saw tears in their eyes. I don't know if I actually believed what I said, but there was something in me that wanted to hurt them and to hurt the beliefs they stood for.

The next day I had to go back to Munich. I shook Kurt's hand and waved Goodbye to all my nieces and nephews. When it came time for me to say Goodbye to Mama and Papa and Friedl, they walked me outside. Papa stood there with a cigar in his mouth, puffing away like he always did so you couldn't tell what he was thinking. When he shook my hand, though, he held on longer than usual and with his other hand grabbed my arm in an embrace. Friedl rubbed my shoulder and said, "We'll stay in touch." Then she had to run into the house because one of her kids had started crying.

When I stood in front of Mama, her eyebrows drew together and tears flowed freely down her face. "My son," she sobbed. She wrapped her arms around me and held me close and then pushed me back so she could look at me. She didn't say much more—I don't think she could speak because of the lump in her throat. She just continued to let the tears flow down her cheeks and looked at my face as though she was memorizing it—as though I was the dearest thing in the world to her. Her heart poured out through her eyes—I will never forget the way she looked. Like a mother hen, she just wanted to pull all her chicks under her wing, and here, one was leaving her to go across the ocean. Touched by her love but ready to go, I turned, waved, and walked toward the train station.

On my last day of work at the bakery in Munich, my boss asked me to write to him when I arrived in America and tell him about the living conditions there. He had heard that immigrants lived in chicken coops for a long time before being integrated into American society. With these encouraging words, I closed the door on my last day at work in Germany.

On October 13, 1956, Else drove me to the train station in Munich, and we waved Goodbye to each other as my train rolled away. I had thought of marrying her, but I knew she would never leave her mother to follow me to America, so we just agreed to go our separate ways.

I didn't think much about saying farewell to Germany as my train rumbled north toward Bremerhaven and the ocean. I had crossed my homeland by train to live in a new town so many times in the past ten years that it seemed only natural to watch the hills and trees roll by, each one separating me farther from Munich and my old life.

The closer the train rolled to the port, the lighter my shoulders became. I was leaving it all behind me—the mess from the war, missed opportunities, broken relationships, my lack of direction, my boring life. I would start over in America: work in a bakery, go to church, maybe even find a good wife. I didn't know what exactly I wanted, just that I would do my best to start over and be a decent person.

America-bound in Bremerhaven, 1956

On October 14, two thousand other refugees and I boarded the USNS *General Harry Taylor,* a wartime U.S. naval transport ship now being used by the Military Sea Transportation Service. It took us ten days of endless ocean—during three of which I was seasick—to reach New York Harbor and the majestic Statue of Liberty. There, we anchored for several hours, signed more papers, and were interrogated one last time to make sure none of us were Nazis. Then we were assigned to groups based on where we were traveling, and I set foot on American soil for the first time—a twenty-six-year-old German refugee with a suitcase in each hand, eighty dollars in my wallet, and a heart full of hope.

CHAPTER EIGHT

American Dreams

When I got on the train headed for Minnesota and my new job, I met Bert, another German refugee. The baker who was sponsoring me was also sponsoring him and his family. With English conversations buzzing confusingly around us, we both were relieved to meet someone who spoke German.

In Minneapolis, our employer, Rudy Wasserman, met us at the train station and, to our relief, greeted us in German. He drove us to Rockford, where his wife welcomed us with a beautiful meal in their home next to the bakery. I learned over dinner that Rudy was five when his family immigrated to the United States and his father began the Rockford Home Bakery that Rudy now ran. It was good to be among fellow Germans.

After dinner, Rudy drove us to our respective houses. I rented a room from the Schaars, a retired farming couple who were also German immigrants. I paid them seventy-five dollars every two weeks for room and board. At the bakery, I made $1.20 an hour for the first six months.

I soon learned that moving across the ocean to America hadn't magically made my life become perfect. While there were many people who spoke German around me, I didn't know them well. Bert was busy with his family, as were all the other people, and without anyone to share my thoughts with every day, I became very lonely. I also was struggling with my work in the bakery. When I arrived in the U.S., I could count only to ten in English, so I found reading the recipes almost impossible at first. I also had a hard time learning the English measurements. I didn't know what pints, quarts, and gallons were or how they related to each other or that sixteen ounces made a pound. Even numbers were a challenge; in Germany, we wrote the number one with a little flag at the top, and we crossed our sevens to differentiate between the two. Here, the numeral one was just a line and the seven didn't have a cross line, so I frequently got those numbers mixed up.

I relied heavily on another single German immigrant, Bernhard, to show me the ropes in the bakery. But soon after I arrived he was drafted into the military. When he left, he asked me to buy his 1950 Chevy. He agreed to take payments, so I gave him five hundred dollars for it.

The wife of my car insurance agent was a retired schoolteacher, and when she heard about the struggles Bert and I were having with English, she offered to teach us for free. She used kindergarten and first-grade books to help us learn to speak, read, and write English, and soon I began to communicate better with the people around me.

I still heard from my loved ones in Germany. When I first arrived in Minnesota, Else and I wrote each other at least twice a week. But over the months our correspondence slowed until it stopped all together. Mama and Friedl also wrote me frequently, telling me news of the family and always encouraging me to rely on Christ. Even Papa wrote me letters once in a while—but only to complain to me about Mama's stubbornness and that she held herself above him in her perfection and that she gave too much money to the evangelicals and that she left him to go to prayer meetings too often. I think he just needed to get his frustrations off his chest.

These letters from home were nice, but as Else faded from my life, I became intensely lonely. I wanted a girl to call my own. I took a girl who worked at the bakery out on a few dates, but the language barrier was a problem and we never really connected. I had also kept in touch with a girl I met on the trip over from Germany, Resi Koller. She settled in Los Angeles with her family, and we wrote each other once in a while to share our experiences as immigrants. When I told her how much I made per hour in Rockford, she wrote back telling me how much bakers made in L.A. I had to work overtime in Rockford to make the same amount.

Lonely and restless after a year in Rockford, I packed my few belongings into my Chevy and headed for L.A. I took my time enjoying the scenery in the states I passed through: the immensity of the plains in Nebraska and Wyoming, the unending height and ruggedness of the Rocky Mountains, the red rocks in Bryce Canyon National Park. The variety and largeness of the American landscape was unlike anything we had in Germany.

In L.A., I got a job that paid eighty-five dollars a week, and I found a furnished room nearby that cost me only a dollar a day. I had hopes of marrying Resi, but soon after I arrived, she announced that she was moving back to Germany and would marry me only if I went back with her. I wasn't about to do that.

In the few weeks that passed between my arrival and Resi's leaving, my landlady told me I should go out with Olga Feener, one of her coworkers. I invited Olga to be my date for a New Year's Eve party. Resi came to that party too—but without a date. I enjoyed dancing all evening with Olga while keeping my eye on Resi—I liked making her jealous. But aside from that, I also began to appreciate Olga's beauty. She was from Colombia, and possessed a South American beauty that was new to me.

Over the next three months, Olga and I spent a lot of time together. I liked having a beautiful girl on my arm again. Her family lived in the area, so we spent many evenings playing bridge with them. I learned a lot about the American lifestyle from them—simple things like how to order pizza and how to play cards.

I was twenty-seven then. I'd been thinking seriously that it was time for me to start a family, so I asked Olga to marry me. She said Yes.

I had big dreams. You come to this country and you think you have to get rich—it's America, right? As I drove Olga home after a celebration dinner with her family, I told her about my dreams. We were holding hands, and both of us had full hearts. "Olga," I said, "I want to have a wonderful life. You know what I want to do? I want to retire when I'm forty-five. I want to work overtime and save all the money possible so we can just relax the rest of our lives. We can take trips around the states, and maybe . . . I don't know. What do you want to do?"

She laughed and shook her head. "Waldemar, I love that idea. I'd like to go on a trip to Hawaii—maybe even see Germany with you."

"OK! We're going to have to work hard to do it. You really want to work hard?"

"I do."

Olga walked down the aisle of a Lutheran church and married me in March of 1958.

Because Olga's father traveled a lot, he stored all of his things in Olga's brother's garage. He had offered us his bedroom set, so shortly after our wedding we went to the garage to get it. While we were digging through things, we found some old family photo albums. When we were dating, Olga had told me that she was the youngest child in her family—about a year younger than me. But as we flipped through the albums, I noticed that in one of the earliest family pictures, she was quite a bit bigger than her brother. I pointed it out: "You look bigger than Joe in this picture."

Olga blushed and stumbled over her reply a bit. "Well, I— I'm actually five years older than you."

What was I to do? She had lied to me, and while it wasn't a big crime, I felt very disappointed. Other things started to show up, too, just as they always do for newlyweds. The perfection and strictness I had been raised with in my home clashed with her way of thinking and acting. For instance, she believed that a woman had the right to be late, which drove me crazy—I believed in being on time or even early. And I always had to be doing something—working on some project, but Olga could sit around for hours and not feel the need to do anything. Still, we were excited that we were beginning our lives together. We enjoyed going on outings: concerts and opera performances at the Hollywood Bowl, including *The Nutcracker*.

Olga became pregnant soon after we married, and we were beside ourselves with excitement the whole nine months. I moved to a higher-paying bakery job, and we bought our first house in September—a small one in Lawndale for nine thousand dollars. We still spent many evenings at her brother's house playing cards, her brother and I drinking together.

When Olga went into labor, we rushed to the hospital in a flurry of excitement. I held her hand in the delivery room, nervous and trembling. I was going to be a father! I finally was getting my life on the right track—a beautiful wife, a new house, a good job, and a sweet little baby.

I stayed next to Olga and encouraged her, but when she had been in labor for twelve hours, we knew something was wrong. The doctor decided to grasp the baby with instruments and pull it out, so Olga's father and I waited outside the delivery room. When the doctor came out into the hall, he looked tired, and his face was a bit pale. "Mr. Leonhardt," he said, "I'm sorry. The baby didn't make it."

I rushed into the room in time to see a nurse handing Olga a still little bundle. She took our baby in her arms, held it close, and cried silently. I put my arms around both of them and felt my heart ache. It was the most pain I had felt in years. I decided to name our little boy Bodo.

While Olga didn't believe in showing her emotions and my heart was still cold from the horrors of war I had seen, the loss of Bodo touched a raw spot in both of us. We cried together several times, and in our grief we drew closer together.

After a few months had passed, we both felt it was time to try to bring another little one into our home, and, on September 10, 1960, Udo Albert was born, a bouncing baby boy. Our beautiful little Nora Esther followed him quickly—she was born on December 31, 1961—and before we knew it, our home was full of sleepless nights and bibs and diapers and lots of love. Olga quit working when the babies came, and I got a job at Oroweat Baking Company, where I received a higher wage than I had ever had before: $4.60 an hour.

Then, in 1963, I started my own drive-in donut shop. It proved to be a great venture. It was near the airport and the Hughes aircraft factory, so customers came in day and night, and I often worked twenty-four hours a day. The business became extremely successful, and I hired girls to tend the counter while I was baking. My success puffed up my ego. That's where I got into trouble.

With the long hours and the great success, I began to think I could do anything I wanted to, and I started flirting with the customers and the girls in my shop. Before long, I was unfaithful to my wife. I'm sorry to this day that I made that choice. It wasn't that I didn't love her. I did. I just had a weak backbone. I always liked to flirt, and then I would flirt myself right into something I didn't have the strength to run away from. Olga was busy with our children, so she couldn't help me much at the shop. That left me alone many hours with the girls who worked the counter.

I had never been able to feel life fully since I saw the carnage outside the train station when I was fourteen. My heart was still cold and numb, so I was always looking for something to stir my emotions. When I was with a woman other than my wife, it wasn't because I loved that woman but because of the rush that being with her gave me. It was all about me.

Mama continued to write me letters. Among the items of news from home she wrote lines that told me of her love for Christ and that she fasted for me regularly. I didn't tell her about my affairs, but often while driving home too late at night,

I could see her nearsighted eyes boring into me as they had when I misbehaved as a child. Just like the eyes in the drawing of Christ that hung on the living-room wall of my childhood home, her intense eyes followed me everywhere and wouldn't let my conscience rest.

Perhaps to fight this image, I bragged about my exploits in my letters to Friedl. I told her about meeting a new woman and going to a hotel with her, and then I wrote, "I know it's wrong, but I like it." I'm sure this hurt Friedl. I'm also sure that I was crying out for attention, though I would never have admitted it. Friedl never responded to these statements. She just kept telling me about their family happenings and encouraging me to ask Christ into my life.

After a year of running the donut shop, I was burned out from all the hard work. So I sold the shop. When we got the money, Olga suggested we use some of it to go to Germany to visit my parents. I told her we didn't have time and needed to use the money for more important things.

We sold our house and bought another one on three-quarters of an acre for $21,500. I got my job at Oroweat back and worked nights there, and although neither Olga nor I paid much attention to religion, something in my conscience made me want our children to have a Christian education. To pay for the private school, I got a job driving the school's bus. For two years, things went on like that: I worked at Oroweat nights and drove the school bus during the day. The only break in the routine was when the Watts riots broke out in 1965, and I had to drive to work past many looted stores. I kept a loaded handgun on the seat next to me, ready to use it if necessary, and my supervisor at Oroweat spent most of the night shifts on the roof with his shotgun. Luckily, neither of us had to use our guns, but we did see the fires against the night sky not far away, and we heard the gunfire.

When the kids started school, I expected that Olga would get a steady job and work toward our goal of retiring at age forty-five, but she didn't. Instead, she got odd jobs here and there. Because I worked day and night, this became very frustrating to me. I didn't feel that Olga was backing me up. On top of that, she didn't support my working so hard. When things would go wrong with my job, she would laugh and say, "I told you so." I wasn't getting the main thing I wanted from our marriage: moral support. I wasn't making much money, so the prospect of reaching my lofty goal of retiring at forty-five was slowly disintegrating before my eyes.

In 1966, Oroweat opened a plant in Beaverton, Oregon, and asked me to help in the mixing department there. Things weren't good between Olga and me at that point, so I agreed. I went home, told her to get herself a job, packed my stuff, kissed the kids Goodbye, and drove north in one of our two cars. I didn't have any plans to come back. In fact, I didn't think much about the future at all; I just knew I had to get out and see something new. I had lived my life that way since I was fourteen—when things got bad, I moved on: to Bavaria when the Russian army invaded, to America when my life lost meaning, to California when I was too lonely in Minnesota, and now to Oregon. I guess I thought running away would make my life better.

While in Oregon, I started to appreciate my married life in a way I never had before. I missed Olga and Udo and Nora, and I called home often. Just before Christmas, I told them I was coming home. I packed my car with tins full of Christmas cookies that I had been baking for months; I added a dog—a German Shepherd mix named Rolf; and I drove away towing a 1956 VW Bug I had just bought.

I arrived home in high spirits, and the kids ran out to meet me. We hugged, and they hugged Rolf, and we all romped around the yard together—kids, Christmas cookies, Rolf, and me. Then I bounded into the house, grinning, with a kid hanging on each arm. I was excited to see Olga. She was sitting at the kitchen table playing cards with a couple of friends. She didn't come and hug me or have a meal prepared. She didn't even get up. She simply said, "Hello."

I got my old night job at Oroweat back again, and we soon slipped into our old routine. The joy of having our family back together lasted only two or three years.

Olga returned to the idea of visiting my parents, but I told her again that we were too busy and needed to take care of our responsibilities. But Mama had the same idea as Olga. In her letters she frequently asked when I would bring my family to meet her. So I figured out a way we could pay for my parents to visit us. We picked a date for them to come and wrote letters back and forth, planning what we would do while they were here, and I started to get excited.

Over the years I had buried my loneliness for my family in hard work, but I really did miss them. When I saw other German immigrant families who had moved here together—mother and father and children and grandkids—I often felt a flash of jealousy and imagined that life was much easier for them because they had extended family to share the burdens. On the nights when I was home and tucked Udo and Nora into their beds, I told them stories about Mama and Papa—how Papa could magically find mushrooms in the forest and how Mama used to punish us by making us pluck feathers.

About a month before my parents were scheduled to visit us, Papa backed out. Even though he had once been in the air force, he didn't want to fly now. "He says the air doesn't have any boards to walk on," Mama wrote. "And I don't think I can come alone. That is an awfully long way to travel alone." I could read her deep disappointment between the lines, and I felt a lump in my throat as I drove to work the night after that letter came.

When I showed the letter to Olga, she said again, "If they won't come here, why don't we go visit them? We have the money now." But I set my sights on another business goal instead. Papa had always shown his love to our family through his hard work. Before he was drafted, he worked all day at his tax job, and when he came home, he worked until midnight chopping wood, fixing our shoes, and taking care of the animals. Though he never had an intimate conversation with me, I knew he loved me because of how hard he worked to provide for our family. That is how I wanted to show my love to my kids.

I thought that if we built some housing units on our property that we could rent out, we would have some extra income and that would make life easier for our family. Construction loans were hard to get because of the Vietnam War and also because we had so little savings, so to work toward this goal, I began working weekends at the El Camino Donut Shop across from El Camino College in Torrance, California. Then the owner began to talk about selling the shop, and I bought it late in 1967.

It turned out to be a good business move. I worked like a mule and built the business up from barely surviving to producing a good living. But it wasn't good for my personal life.

Just as before, I often worked around the clock, and beautiful college girls came in at all hours. I hired a beautiful, twenty-four-year-old girl to tend the counter, and before long I had flirted myself into an affair with her. Soon I was flirting with all the female employees and sometimes going out with them, so they vied with each other for my attention. This stroked my ego.

Then I hired Nina Rawlings, a nineteen-year-old whose father had just passed away. She needed a job to help her mother financially. I was thirty-seven, and she was nineteen. The first time I went out with her, I was just on a power trip; it was all about my ego and had nothing to do with her. I just did it to prove that I could capture the attention of one more girl. But then she was so young, and she made it so easy for me to get what I wanted that we got together more and more frequently until she was my steady companion and she said she loved me. As before, I was working long hours at the donut shop—frequently all night. So I easily got away with staying out with Nina.

Back then I didn't think; I just did what I wanted to do. I felt responsible for my kids and my marriage, so I didn't want Olga to find out about my affairs, but I didn't care enough to stop having them. Even the thought of Mama's piercing, disappointed eyes couldn't stop me from walking down the destructive path I was on.

Mama had to stay in bed most of the time now because of extreme hardening of the arteries, so Papa did most of the letter-writing. When Mama did write, her script was shaky and weak, yet her letters were always positive. She was thankful that my brother Kurt and his wife, Wally, were so generous as to take care of her in their home. I read each letter with a twinge of guilt that I couldn't help care for them, and then I tossed the letter aside as I went back to work.

As Olga and I grew further apart, I filled in the gaps in my life with lots of work and with other women. I no longer dreamed of building those rental units on our property or of retiring at forty-five. I didn't work with thoughts of my kids constantly in my mind. I just drowned myself in pleasures.

Olga had been jealous since the beginning of our marriage, always trying to catch me looking at some other woman long before I was unfaithful to her. Now, somehow, she learned about my relationship with Nina. One morning when I went home to sleep, she followed me into our bedroom and shut the door. "I know about Nina," she said.

I opened a drawer, pulled some pants out, stuffed them in my duffel bag, and walked past her to the door even though I had just gotten there.

She grabbed my arm. "You know what I'll have to do if you don't stop, don't you?" she said.

"I have to go back to work," I countered. Then I jerked my arm out of her grasp and walked out the door.

Within a couple days, I found a room to rent halfway between the donut shop and my home. I moved into it, and Nina started spending many more nights with me. I hardly went home anymore, and when Olga and the kids came to the donut shop, I didn't give her much of a chance to talk with me. I didn't want to talk to her. I just wanted to keep doing what I felt like doing. I didn't think about how my actions were ruining my family.

A couple weeks later, I got a letter from Olga's lawyer saying she was filing for a divorce and that I should get a lawyer, too, so I did. When Olga filed the divorce papers, the state said we could have free counseling. She wanted to try it, but I refused. I was too stubborn.

In the meantime, Nina had moved in with me. Then one day, I decided to leave her. I packed up my things and told her, "I'm too old for you, and we have different ideas about life."

It was true. We didn't have much in common except for wanting to escape from our lives. But she begged me to stay. She clung to my arm and said, "Don't go. I love you."

"No," I said, "I have to go." I was firm. I took my things and walked out the door. As I walked away, she opened the window, crying and yelling, "I love you! I love you!"

I didn't even feel touched at all. I was just glad to get out— I had never intended to stay with her.

That lasted only a couple of days—until I had to go back to work, and she was there. Several days later we got back together.

CHAPTER NINE

Desert Nightmare

After Olga filed for divorce, I worked as hard as I could, and when I wasn't working, I drowned myself in my relationship with Nina. Soon, though, that became monotonous. So, in August of 1969, I finally stopped to think about my actions. My back and feet ached all the time because of the baking I did around the clock to fulfill customers' demands. I had to pay child support and alimony and make the house payments even though I couldn't live in the house anymore. I was thirty-eight years old and had a twenty-year-old girlfriend. And my children were growing up without me. I felt like my life was useless.

One night, I worked till dawn alone in the shop baking the next day's donut batch. In the morning, I slumped over the counter with my head in my hands while I waited for Nina to come in and take over the shop. She bounced in at seven-thirty and came straight to me. She threw her arms around me from behind and stretched up to kiss me.

I grunted and jerked my head away from her, throwing her arms off and straightening up at the same time. "I'm going home," I said, and I unlocked the cash register to take out the surplus cash from the receipts of the past twenty-four hours.

"What's the matter with you?" Nina asked.

I didn't reply. I didn't want to engage with her that day. She had nothing that I wanted.

As I gathered my coat and the dirty aprons to take home, she followed me around the shop, trying to get my attention. But I pushed her away every time she came close. Finally, she sat down on the stool behind the cash register and pulled her hair up into a high ponytail, watching me the whole while. "You know, Waldy," she said, slowly pulling off her sweatshirt as I headed to the door, "I'm young enough." Her voice taunted me. "I don't have to stay with you. I can leave anytime I want to and find another man. I'm young enough."

I turned my head toward the door and said nothing in return, but my eyes stung and I felt empty as I opened the car door. She was right. I didn't own her. I didn't own anybody. When it came down to it, I was alone. No one needed anything but my money.

As I drove the short distance to our apartment, I felt pressure build up in my head. *I'll let it all go, just let it all go. I can let the house payment go and the business and Nina, and I'll be free.*

When I got to the apartment, I stuffed four hundred dollars into my wallet and packed a change of clothes and the bottle of Valium my doctor had prescribed for me. I scribbled a note on a piece of paper, drove by my house, and stuffed it in the mailbox. The note read: "I hereby give Olga Leonhardt the rights to all possessions of Waldemar Leonhardt. Signed, Waldemar H. Leonhardt, 7 August 1969."

I merged onto Interstate 605 and headed east to find a place where I could lie down, take my Valium pills, and die. I couldn't think, and I couldn't feel anything but the pounding pressure in my head, like the sensation chronic migraine sufferers describe. All I could do was press the accelerator down.

Miles and miles of desert passed, and I just kept driving. I wanted to find somewhere to lie down and die, but I was too tired even to expend the effort to stop the car and find a suitable place. My foot stayed on the accelerator and my hands kept the wheel straight as I moved through the sandy brown world. By now I had been up for almost thirty hours, and I just wanted to lie down and fall asleep and not feel anything ever again. Just to fall asleep.

As the sun fell low in the sky, I noticed something glimmering on the horizon. My foggy mind registered that it must be Las Vegas that was rising out of the desert and reflecting the sun's rays. I hadn't meant to go to Las Vegas.

My desperately tired mind somehow got me to the parking lot of a hotel on the edge of the city, and I pulled in and paid for a room. Before going up to it, I fumbled with the change in my pocket and somehow clinked some coins into the slot in the lobby pay phone.

"Olga? I want you to go to the donut shop and get whatever you want. It's all yours—flour, sugar, whatever you need." Even in my stupor, I felt responsible for Olga and the children. After all, we were still married. She should take what she wanted of the business.

"I got your note in the mailbox, Waldemar. Where are you?"

I ignored her question and said, "Maybe you shouldn't take all the money in the cash register, though. The waitresses can have that to pay their day's wage. Will that be all right?"

"Well, I need some money to take Udo to the doctor. He's had a stomachache for over a week now, and I'm getting worried, and I don't have any extra cash."

"I'll send some for you. Don't worry, but don't take the money in the cash register, OK?"

I hung up and shuffled over to the hotel lobby desk. "Do you have an envelope I can use?" I asked. I stuffed fifty dollars in the envelope and scribbled our address on it. "Please mail this tomorrow," I told the attendant. She nodded and put her hand out.

"Ah, postage."

I fumbled in my pocket, pulled out six cents, and plunked them on the counter. Then I trudged out of the lobby and walked down the row of worn hotel-room doors until I reached my room. When I got inside, I fell onto the bed and pulled the bottle of Valium pills out of my pocket. This would be as good a place as any to end it all, and I was ready—I had taken care of Olga and the children.

I poured half the pills into my palm and looked at them. Then a sharp memory jabbed through my clouded brain, piercing the pressure that pushed against the front of my forehead tighter than a piping bag full of frosting. *Mama.* She was sick, bedridden. It would kill her if I died.

I couldn't think anymore that day. I poured all but one of the pills back in the bottle, tossed that pill down my throat, and flopped my head onto the pillow. And I didn't move again until I had slept eight hours.

When I woke in the morning, the pressure in my head was gone. In its place, I felt a sharp pain in my chest—disappointment that I was awake for another day. I wanted to die. I had no reason to be alive. I had no relationship in my life worth staying alive for. The only thing my days accomplished was the baking of another batch of flour, water, and sugar into round lumps that people stuck into their mouths. I didn't want to see the end of this day.

Putting the bottle of pills into my pocket and getting in the car again, I passed quickly through downtown Las Vegas and headed east into the white morning sun and an even more desolate desert.

With each mile that passed, I looked for a large pile of rocks or a bush big enough to lie down behind, where I could take my pills and not feel anything anymore. When I saw a big pile of rocks ahead, I slowed my car to pull off the road. But the sharp thought that had pricked me the night before returned: *Mama. It'll kill Mama.*

I sped up again, and the thought rolled through my mind: *I want to die. I want to die. I want to die.*

I had to struggle just to breathe. I forced each breath out so hard that I thought my lungs would collapse.

I just want to die. But I can't kill Mama.

Each time I slowed the car to pull over, the thought of her filled my brain. My heart hurt just as badly thinking about her as it did thinking about myself. I remembered watching her sob in her bedroom when Walter died and knowing that her heart had broken. I remembered how she sang around the house less and less frequently after the telegram about Erwin came. I remembered her dull emptiness at the loss of Manfred and Edmund, and how she drew me to her the last time I saw her—her hand caressing the back of my head, her tears streaming down her cheeks, how she held onto me as if she would never let me go.

As the sun climbed higher in the sky and glinted off the white salty sands of Utah, I followed highway 15 higher and higher and still saw only barren desert—miles of sand and brush and rock. *No one would know who I am. I could lie down and the sand would be cool against my ear and I would just fall asleep. Oh, please let me lie down.*

I pulled the car over and stopped completely. There was a

big rock not too far off the road. I got the Valium out. My head still buzzed from the vibration of the road I had been rumbling over for hours.

It would be so nice not to feel anymore, I thought. *So nice not to feel. I want to die.*

But a voice still argued with me. *And kill your mother?*

It was the voice of my German upbringing—guilt, but also tenderness. My mother had done nothing but care for me.

I want to die.

And kill your own mother?

I saw her lying in bed, body stiff in pain, thinking only of me and Friedl and Kurt as she waited for each day to pass.

I want to die.

It almost seemed to me that I could feel her hand on my arm, and then I heard her words echo in my head—the words she had spoken that morning at the train station in Sprottau as she pulled me away from the soldier: "You stay with me. You are the last one. You stay with me." Her voice was frantic yet firm. "You are the last one."

I turned the key again and got back on the freeway, and the argument filled the entire day. Was my will to die stronger than my mother's voice? I imagined Papa walking into Mama's sickroom and telling her the news of another dead son, and her dying from the grief, and I just couldn't do it.

I made it to Salt Lake City as the sun turned the air golden again. I drove on streets bustling with people and found another hotel, a little nicer this time. I had a couple of beers in the hotel bar and then headed upstairs and sat down on the bed. For the first time in several days, I began to breathe smoothly. I closed my eyes and leaned back against the wall. *Maybe I could start all over. Maybe I could just get a job and start over where no one needs me. Maybe I don't have to die to leave it all behind me.*

I dozed off to sleep and woke in the morning with that thought going through my head: *I'll start all over. I'll just get a job out here.*

I recognized the feeling: the hope of starting over that I had felt in Germany when I decided to immigrate, in Minnesota when I moved to California, in California when I moved to Oregon. Moving somewhere else would make everything OK. All I needed to be a good person, to find meaning, was a fresh start away from everything familiar.

That day I applied for a job at Peter Pan Bakeries in Salt Lake City. With my experience, they hired me on the spot and told me I could start the next day. I went back to the hotel room and within the hour changed my mind. I called them, told them to forget it, and hit the road again, still traveling northeast.

This journey east was just the reverse of the one I had driven twelve years earlier—but then I was full of hope for a rich American life. Now, I had less than three hundred fifty dollars left in my pocket after twelve years of hard work building businesses, I had left a string of broken promises in my wake. And I was nowhere close to being the responsible citizen I had envisioned myself becoming. All my hopes for fulfillment had led to dead ends, and whenever I thought of God now, which wasn't often, I knew He condemned me; I knew for certain I was lost forever. If I thought I was bad as a kid, I now knew I was the worst of sinners with no hope for redemption. Still, I thought that if I could start over, I could at least live the rest of my life appearing to be a good person. Maybe I could live in a community where I didn't harm everyone in my path with my selfishness. I wanted to be a good person.

And what better way to be a good person than to get a job? I passed through the high plains of the Rocky Mountains and watched the harsh sagebrush gradually change to soft prairie grass as I neared Cheyenne, Wyoming. As evening approached, I suddenly realized how hungry I was. During the past three days, I hadn't eaten much more than a small bag of peanuts and some crackers I had bought at a gas station. So, I stopped at a small bakery just outside Cheyenne.

"Hello," I said as I opened the door and the bell jangled. An elderly man behind the counter looked up and gave me a polite nod. I asked for a roll and pulled out some change. After exchanging the money for the roll, I stayed in the shop and watched the old clerk checking out of the cash register, preparing to close for the day. Leaning against the counter, I asked, "So, is business good in this part of the country?"

He mumbled and nodded, eyeing me out of the corner of his eye.

"What chances are there that I could work in a local retail bakery?"

He cleared his throat and straightened up. "I don't know," he said, his voice a little edgy.

"Do you need any help here? I could help you." I opened my hands as I made the offer.

The old man backed up, feeling the door behind the counter with his hands. His eyes were wide, and he fumbled for the doorknob.

"I'm just wondering if you might need some help."

"Yes, no. Uh, I don't know. I need to close up," he said and opened the door. Realizing that he was frightened, I turned and went back to my car.

I stopped at the hotel that night still puzzling over why that man had seemed so scared. When I turned on the light and looked in the mirror, the reason was clear: I had five days' growth of beard and was pale and scruffy, unshowered and travel-weary, my cheeks were sunken in and my eyes blood-shot. And it was clear I hadn't eaten much for a few days.

The next morning I shaved, ate a good breakfast, and then drove all day, which put me in Omaha, Nebraska, right about dinnertime. I ate another good meal, and the next day sent Olga another fifty dollars and applied for a job at a retail bakery. They told me I could start the following day.

That evening, I scanned the newspaper's help wanted section and found an opening for a baker in Norfolk, Nebraska, about 115 miles northwest. That sounded like the perfect place to start my life again—away from the big cities, in the country. I had a good feeling about it. I called the bakery and again was instantly offered the job, on condition that the personal interview went well. The pay was $125 per week instead of the $95 I would have made in Omaha.

As soon as I decided to start over in Norfolk, I felt an urge to call Olga and ask her to come there too. I wanted to fix things. Still a stranger in America without any relatives here, I didn't want to lose every relationship I had built. I didn't want to be completely alone.

The nearest pay phone was four blocks down the hill. As I loafed down the sidewalk, I thought, *I should call Nina,* and the rest of the way to the phone, I flip-flopped back and forth. Nina. Olga. Nina. Olga. I was still undecided when I stood in front of the phone with the receiver in my hand. I knew the phone where Nina and I lived had been disconnected, but I could call her sister Gerry to see if Nina was at her house. I decided that was the best way to make my decision—I would call Gerry's, and if Nina wasn't there, I would call Olga.

Nina was there.

"Nina? Hi. How are you?"

"I'm fine," she said. "I've got my car packed up to leave for Oregon tomorrow."

"Oh, yeah?"

"Yeah. I'm going to go up to Hood River to stay with my brother for a while."

"Huh," I said. "Well, I just called to tell you that if you want to be with me, you'll have to come to Nebraska."

"*Nebraska!* What are you doing in Nebraska?"

"That's where I am. I can buy you a ticket to fly here."

She was quiet for a second. Then she said, "OK, I'll come."

The next morning I wired her the airline ticket, and I picked her up at the airport the following day. From the airport, we drove straight to Norfolk to interview and, hand in hand, introduced ourselves as husband and wife. I started work the next day. We rented a small, furnished basement, and Nina found a job as a waitress at a truck stop.

Within a week I got promoted to foreman at higher pay. Hertha Huber, one of the women who helped in the bakery, spoke German, and we became fast friends. I learned that her mother had come from Bunzlau, Silesia, only about twenty-five miles from where I was born.

Through Hertha and her husband, Nina and I met many good, old-fashioned, Lutherans. They all thought we were married, and we let them believe that. They had strict Christian standards, and I tried to match the way I lived my life to theirs. They were a good influence on both Nina and me.

Before long, one of the members of the German community put a beautiful big house up for rent, so Nina and I moved into it. About a month after we arrived in Norfolk, Nina started having morning sickness, and on June 13, 1970, our son Edmund Ray was born. Although neither Nina nor I believed in infant baptism, to fit in with our friends we had him baptized into the Lutheran church. We were living a hypocritical life, but for the first time in many years, I felt I had the respect of a good community that would have made my father proud.

On December 23, 1970, I told Nina we should get married, and on December 24, she, Edmund, and I drove an hour and a half to Fremont, Nebraska, to be married in secret by the justice of the peace there. Now, we could live together with clean consciences. A year later, we bought the Westgate Teahouse, a small family restaurant with forty-eight seats. Just a little more than two years after my desert nightmare, I had a new life with a wife, a baby boy, good Christian friends, and the prospects of a good business. I had made a new start.

CHAPTER TEN

Father's Son

A month after we bought the Westgate Teahouse, I was frying some hamburgers for a family who came in early for dinner, during the slow part of the afternoon. I flipped the burgers, pressed them down with the spatula, and watched the pink flesh turn dark brown. Then Nina walked into the kitchen holding an envelope. I slid the finished burgers onto the plate where the buns and lettuce were already waiting and said, "Hi, dear. I didn't expect you to be here."

"This letter came in the mail today," she said. "It looks important."

I took the letter from her and saw that it was from Germany. As Nina watched, I tore open the envelope and read the letter. Mama had died. She had passed away several days before. Instantly, my eyes filled with tears. I was stunned. I hadn't seen Mama in the sixteen years since I left Germany, yet the thought of her had kept me alive.

I blew my nose. When I looked up, I saw that Evelyn, our waitress, had walked in. Both she and Nina were watching me, obviously concerned.

"My mother . . . My mother . . . She passed away."

"I'm sorry," Evelyn said. Then she rushed the plates with the burgers out to the customers.

When Evelyn left, Nina gave me a long hug. Then she said that she had left the car running and needed to turn it off, and she left.

I leaned against the counter, struggling to believe that my mother, who had always been the one steady force in my life, was dead—and I hadn't gone to see her and to say Goodbye. Olga had asked me over and over to go and visit Mama, but I hadn't listened. Now the thought that she was gone hurt me like a stab in the chest. Oh, how I wished I could see her again. (I later found out that Olga had taken Udo and Nora to visit my family in Germany just after our divorce, so Mama did get to meet two of my kids before she died.)

As I stood there, the bell on the door jingled several times, and before long, Evelyn brought in the orders of three more families. But the tears in my eyes made it difficult for me to fill the orders. Memory after memory flooded my brain: Mama letting me eat the whole jar of strawberries before we fled Sprottau; her holding on to me in the train station; her always finding food for me when I came to visit in Bavaria even though she didn't have enough herself; her doing my laundry when I rode the train and then walked nine miles home from my bakery apprenticeship every weekend. Her faithfulness to God during all the hard times she had lived through: when one son after another was killed, and when Papa and her son-in-law were in the war, and when she was forced from her home. She still had hope because she had faith in God. I thought of her singing in that sweet voice and fasting for me regularly after I left home—always hopeful, always holding on to God.

When Nina had turned off the car engine, she came to help me in the kitchen. And when she saw how emotional I was, she sent me home.

I soon buried my sorrow in my work. Business lagged for the first year after we opened the restaurant. But when I added German food and pastries and played some German background music, it picked up. Soon, German GI brides, immigrants, and people of German descent came from as far as fifty miles away to taste familiar food.

Halfway through that year, Friedl wrote that she and Siegfried were planning to visit the U.S., and they wondered whether they could spend some time with us. Of course, we said Yes.

They stayed with us for a week. Nina and I soon learned to change the subject quickly when Siegfried began to talk about religion. He used the Bible as a hammer, and we didn't want to hear any of it. Still, their faithfulness to their Adventist beliefs impressed me. They kept Saturday as a day of rest and didn't eat what I thought of as normal food because of their religious convictions. Seeing my sister did warm my heart, but Nina and I considered her religious beliefs a bunch of baloney.

In the December after our first year at the Westgate Teahouse, we closed the restaurant for three weeks, and Nina, Edmund, and I flew to Germany to see my father. He was eighty-three, and I didn't want to miss the chance to see him before he died as I had my mother.

Papa was happy to see me, but we didn't really talk much. The night we arrived, he offered me some gin. I pulled out a bottle of whiskey I had brought from America, and Papa, my brother Kurt, and I bragged ourselves into a drinking contest. Papa drank pretty heavily on a regular basis; it numbed him so he didn't have to think about anything from the past that he didn't want to. I don't remember even talking about Mama while we were there. We just drank and played chess and ate together and enjoyed being near each other.

After Christmas, my little family left Kurt and Papa's house for a few days to visit other relatives. Both Edmund and Nina, who was pregnant and had morning sickness, came down with such bad colds that they had to stay in bed. When I felt myself getting a sore throat, I decided we'd better go home early. I got the airline to change our flight and then left Nina and Edmund with our relatives while I went back to Kurt's house to collect the rest of our things.

I stayed overnight with Kurt and Papa and had some drinks and a couple meals there. When I stood up to leave after breakfast the next morning, I felt closer to Papa than I had ever felt before. Other than the day he came back from the war, he never shared his feelings freely and didn't let anyone close to him, so I had never had really strong feelings for him. But when I stood at the door with my luggage, I felt a huge lump come to my throat and tears come to my eyes. I had the feeling that I wouldn't see him again. I turned my head, walked to the car, and didn't say much more as I loaded the trunk. I think he understood.

While I was in Germany, I got into some pretty heavy conversations with my family about the Vietnam War. They had a lot of negative things to say about America and how we were making a mess of the world. Even though I couldn't say many good things about the Vietnam War, I found myself defending the United States, calling it my country. I didn't realize how American I was until that trip.

When our plane landed at Chicago O'Hare airport, Nina and I looked out the window and saw a huge American flag blowing wide open in the breeze. I decided right there that I wanted to become an American citizen. After a couple years of classes, I said the Pledge of Allegiance in front of a judge and became an American citizen in Omaha, Nebraska, on October 7, 1974.

Our daughter, Rhonda Marie, had been born the previous year, on July 6, 1973. About that time our restaurant business really took off, and by the beginning of 1975, I felt pretty good about myself. We still had our Lutheran friends, we had two beautiful children, we were making good money, and I had become an American citizen.

Then, as had happened in California, our success started to go to my head. I started to flirt with the high school girls we had hired as waitresses, and I couldn't keep my hands to myself. My downfall was a young woman named Linda who worked next door. Even though my relationship with Nina was going well and she was very supportive of my business, when opportunities presented themselves, I didn't resist the temptation.

One afternoon, I bought a gift for Linda, wrapped it up, and stuck it in the back seat of my car. When I went home to take the nap I always took between the lunch and dinner rushes, I covered the present with a jacket so Nina wouldn't see it. Then I went inside and lay down on the bed.

Meanwhile, Nina took our St. Bernard puppy, Rufus, out for a walk. When they got into the front yard, he went straight to my car and began sniffing at the doors. Nina called him to come back, but he wouldn't listen. Finally, she went over to see what he could be so interested in, and she found the present and the note I had written to Linda.

I woke from my nap with Nina shaking my shoulder. "Waldy. I found this in your car," she said. "What's going on with Linda?"

Assuming she thought the present and note were for a waitress named Linda, I said, "You don't think I'm after Linda, do you? She's not my type at all—so tall."

But Nina said, "I know exactly which Linda this is."

So Nina knew about the girl next door. I didn't know what to say or do.

Nina came over, knelt by the bed, and asked, "How could you do this to me?" Then she began to sob as if her heart were being squeezed out of her chest, and she repeated the words "I don't know how you could do this to me" over and over.

I watched her cry for a minute or two, but I didn't touch her or say anything. I didn't know what to do. I couldn't comfort her because I'd been the one who had made her cry.

Then I thought of an out. "Nina," I said, breaking into her crying, "if you would have lost some weight and would have given me what I wanted when I wanted it, I wouldn't have had to do this. But what's a man supposed to do? *You* made me look at other women. It's really *your* fault. You could have chosen to keep me all to yourself."

Nina gasped as if someone had punched her in the stomach and then she sobbed harder.

Of course, what I'd said was all a lie. I had made it up on the spot. Nina was young and beautiful. The problem was that I didn't have the guts to take the blame.

Scooting to the foot of the bed, I said, "I have to get back to the restaurant for dinner," and I walked out the door. I had no idea what to do about it or how to take responsibility, so I just left with Nina's cries of, "How could you do this to me?" following me out the door. I knew I didn't want to lose her. I didn't want to leave her. We had built too much together.

That night, when I went home after closing the restaurant, Nina was still sobbing. That made me angry. I stood in the living room with my hands on my hips, still holding my coat in one hand, and watched her cry.

"What do you want?" I finally barked though I had a lump in my throat. "Do you want me to stay or to leave? It's your choice."

Nina kept crying and shook her head. She didn't know.

"What do you want? You choose," I barked more loudly.

She still didn't answer.

This time I yelled. "Do you want me to leave?"

She just sobbed quietly.

I threw my coat to the floor and stormed to the kitchen, swung open the refrigerator door, and found a half-empty bottle of wine. I was desperate. I hated her for not throwing me out, and I hated her for not begging me to stay. But really, I hated myself. I had messed it all up again, ruined my chance to have a good life.

I grabbed the bottle of wine, swallowed most of its contents, and then banged the bottle back down on the counter. My restraint loosened by the alcohol, I grabbed the dining-room table, picked it up, and smashed it to the floor upside down. Then I picked up one of the chairs and slammed it against the table and the floor, breaking it into splinters. I grabbed another chair and pounded it against the floor until I held only a leg in my hand. And then I did the same to the other two chairs.

The washing machine and dryer were in a little room off the

kitchen, and I went after them, too, pulling them off the wall and pushing them into another wall, their feet screeching on the linoleum floor. I tried to push the refrigerator out from the wall too, but I couldn't move it. My mind started to clear, so I grabbed the bottle, took the last swig of liquid left in it, and with a pumping head and pounding heart, stormed from our home to the Teahouse, leaving Nina standing in the living room.

I woke up at 3:00 A.M. on the linoleum floor of the Teahouse kitchen. My body ached all over from my blow-up at home and from sleeping half a night on that cold, hard floor. I got up, started the griddles for the morning pancakes, and cooked anyway. Then, angry at the whole world, I decided to go to a lawyer and file for a divorce. I didn't think much about it, I just assumed that was what I should do.

I thought I hated Nina, but it was really myself whom I hated. From an early age, I had believed that if you do bad things, you don't deserve love, and I thought I had placed myself in that category many years before. I'd been able to project the image of being a good person for several years, but now that Nina had discovered my affair, it was over.

I went to the law office after the morning breakfast rush and told the lawyer the whole thing—that I'd had an affair, and that I wanted to get a divorce and I wanted our things to be divided equally this time. I didn't want to lose everything I had worked for as I had the last time. I'm not sure what else I wanted— probably to be in control by being the one to file for the divorce, to be the one who decided what would happen.

The lawyer listened calmly with folded hands, and when I stopped talking, he leaned back in his chair with a sigh. "Tell you what," he said. "I want you to go home and think about this for a couple of days, just let it cool off. Then, if you still want the divorce, you can come back and I'll help you get it done."

I hung my head for several seconds and then looked back up. "OK," I said. "I'll give it a few days. Thank you for your time."

I went back to the restaurant, and Nina called me there and said that it was my choice whether to leave or not, but that she wanted me to know that when I smashed up the furniture, a splinter had struck her eye and she had to go see the eye doctor.

I felt bad about that. Then I had a new thought: *What if I went home and asked Nina's forgiveness?* I didn't want to throw away our life together. That afternoon I drove home and practically fell on my knees asking her to forgive me.

She did forgive me, and that was the end of it. I was always faithful to her after that.

In that same year, 1975, several franchise restaurants opened in the neighborhood, and business slowed at the Teahouse. And with the same girls still hanging around, Nina felt uncomfortable even though I didn't so much as lift a finger in their direction. So, we decided to close the Teahouse and start over in Minnesota.

We stored all our belongings in a friend's barn, packed up the basic necessities in our two cars, and set off on the highway. For a month we stayed with friends, and then we camped while we looked for jobs. We finally found jobs in Blaine, Minnesota, and bought a mobile home in a trailer park there. I was starting from scratch again, although I had Nina, Edmund, and Rhonda with me this time.

In 1976, Kurt wrote to tell me Papa had passed away. I didn't feel much when I got the news. I had known that our visit a few years before was our last one.

A couple of years and a couple of jobs later, Baldinger Baking Company in St. Paul hired me, and I worked there for the next fourteen years. I needed a job with good health insurance and a pension plan for retirement, and Baldinger provided that. In 1978, we bought another mobile home, this time in Landfall, just east of St. Paul, and moved there.

While my new job at Baldinger offered good benefits, the work was hard. Though the bakery aimed at high production, it used obsolete equipment, which meant extra work for employees. I was a supervisor, but I had a hard time getting along with some of the other supervisors. When I suggested more efficient ways to do things, they became angry and fought me, always wanting to be right. I often worked long hours of overtime when no one else was there. Our shifts were constantly changed, so I never knew what to expect. On top of that, Nina was switching jobs, so I had to carry the entire burden of family finances. At forty-eight, this life was far from the retirement my twenty-eight-year-old self had predicted I would already be enjoying.

I brought my stress home. I was short-tempered and mean with my family, and I drank too much most evenings. I thought the hard work I did to care for my family excused my harsh words.

One night I came home from an especially hard day of butting heads with another supervisor. When I walked in the door, the smell of dinner hung in the air, three dirty plates sitting on the table told me my family had finished eating, and I didn't see any food left for me. There was a pile of clean, unfolded laundry on the couch, and Nina and the kids and our German shepherd, Cindy, were all wrestling on the floor. Nina was tickling both of the kids on their tummies, and they were all laughing deep belly laughs.

The scene would have warmed the heart of almost any father, but it enraged me. "Where's my dinner, and why isn't that laundry folded?" I barked, and my voice got louder as I went on. "You think you can roll around on the floor not doing anything when there's so much work to be done? You lazy woman! You lazy kids! Can't you do anything right when I'm not here?"

Edmund and Rhonda, who were nine and six at the time, looked at me with wide, scared eyes and then ran to their rooms. Nina stared at me a second or two longer and then turned and followed the kids. And Cindy, the only one left in the room, put her tail between her legs and, without making eye contact with me, followed Nina.

When I was alone, my anger turned into sadness that weighed heavily on my chest. *What have I done?* I thought. The wide eyes of my kids burned in my brain—they showed how deeply my words had hurt them. In fifteen seconds, I had turned a room full of light and laughter into a dark place of fear—so dark that not even the dog would stay with me.

The looks on the faces of my children reminded me of something. I couldn't put my finger on it at first. It was something that had happened long ago. And then I had it. I was back in the kitchen of the house where I was born, and my brothers and I were trapped behind the table while my father slapped Mama and yelled in her face about what an awful woman she was. I couldn't escape, so I had to hear each cruel word and feel the hard slap of flesh against flesh in my little seven-year-old heart.

I had vowed then never to hit a woman, and I had kept that vow. But now I realized that my raging at my family had just the same effect. I was turning into my father, and I knew I had to find a way to stop that from happening. I realized that it wasn't the world around me that needed to change—I was the one who needed to change. So I started to read the Bible. I usually had a glass of wine or a bottle of beer in my hand, but I did start to read.

In the summer, when I got home from a stressful day at work, I often went out to Tanner's Lake, just a few blocks away from us. I would swim out to the middle of the lake and float on my back, the water around my ears blocking out all sounds but my own heartbeat.

One day as I lay on my back and looked at the sky, with wisps of cloud drifting by, I began to realize that my family needed something to hold onto. For many years, I had ignored the thought of God, but the knowledge was still there, strong from my childhood. I knew there was a God watching over us, and a heaven and a hell, and Christ and the devil. I had never stopped believing in these things—I just thought there was no hope for me so I didn't pay much attention to them.

I still didn't believe there was hope for me: I had lied, cheated, stolen, and committed adultery, and I never kept the Sabbath holy. Still, I began to believe that there could be hope for my family, and that giving them something to hold onto would be worth the effort.

I had rarely seen my father pray. I remember only his mumbling a prayer at Christmas with his pipe in his mouth. I hadn't thought I needed to pray either, but out there in the middle of the lake, I sent up my first prayer in decades: *Dear God, please take*

care of Nina and Edmund and Rhonda. Please be with Udo and Nora in
California too. Please help them all to follow the right path. Please give
them something to hold onto. In the name of Your Son, amen.

Three years before, Olga had gotten in touch with me, and
I was able to see Udo and Nora for the first time in six or seven
years. They were growing up—teenagers. On their first visit
to Minnesota, Nora had asked me to tuck her in at night, and I
realized how much I had deprived her of when I left. As we
spent more time together, Udo started asking me for fatherly
advice, and I cherished his trust. I wanted them to have good
lives; I wanted to make up for the pain I had caused them.

I never dared to pray for myself, but I prayed the same prayer
over and over for Nina and my children—that God would
somehow get them on the right track. Through my Bible reading, I started to change. Even though I had no hope that I would
be saved, I wanted to show my family a good life.

I told Edmund and Rhonda that they should pray every night
before going to sleep, and when they said they didn't know what
to say, I wrote them a prayer, which they soon knew by heart:

I have worked and played all day.
Now I go to bed and pray.
Father, I don't see You, but I know You are here
'Cause the Bible tells me You are always near.
Please keep Your watchful eyes open for me
So that no harm will come when I sleep and can't see.

Nina was watching me. On holidays, I wrote her love poems
and tried to show her how much I appreciated the love she gave
me. One day, while I was reading the Bible, she came up behind

me, put her hands on my shoulders, and bent around to kiss my cheek. When I looked up at her, she said, "Why don't we go to church?"

That did it. We searched for a year. We started by watching *The Hour of Power* on TV, and then we tried different churches on Sundays. Finally, we chose the United Pentecostal Church. We didn't know much about doctrines, but the friendliness of the people drew us in. They didn't pressure us to be anything but ourselves, so we stayed. Little did I know that I wouldn't be able to rest there.

CHAPTER ELEVEN

The Living Room

Children grow up so fast. Before we knew it, Edmund and Rhonda were in their early teens. Both Nina and I had full-time jobs, but we tried to arrange our hours so that for the most part one of us was home when the other was working. And we all went to church regularly as a family.

Still, our children spun out of control. Edmund started running away from home at the age of eleven. He said he ran away because no one loved him. He eventually got involved in drugs and then married when he was eighteen.

Rhonda followed in Edmund's footsteps, running away from home for the first time at the age of sixteen, when she became infatuated with a boy. One day, when we had found her and brought her back home, I punched my fist through a window because she said she was going to run away again as soon as I left to go to the grocery store. I was furious that I couldn't control either of my children.

I did care deeply about them. I tried to raise them by the principles with which my parents brought me up, which included showing my love by taking care of their material needs and not so much by hugs and kisses. Apparently, that didn't communicate my love adequately.

In 1987, Friedl and Siegfried invited me to visit them in Australia when their family was having a reunion. Friedl was seventy-three and had already had several strokes, and I wanted to spend time with her before her health got worse, so I went.

When Friedl and Siegfried met me at the airport, I picked her up off the ground and spun her around in a circle. Both of us were laughing, we were so happy to be together again. I felt something like the way I had felt when we connected again in Goerlitz after I got lost in the train station. Life had given us both a few knocks, but for a few moments the joy of being together again erased all of them. When Siegfried and I argued about doctrines, Friedl spoke softly and reminded us to treat each other with love.

Back at home, my relationship with Nina was deteriorating at the same time Edmund and Rhonda were spinning out of control. Nina had always been the better person of the two of us—she had never been unfaithful to me and had always tried to pull our family together. But under the influence of her new Pentecostal friends, things changed.

Nina became deeply involved in the Pentecostal church. When we first began to attend, I found this attractive. The members were friendly and down to earth. Then, one day when the pastor's wife was visiting in our home, she told Nina that women could have separate checking accounts from their husbands. That marked the beginning of the end of our marriage. Money troubles began to damage our relationship. I tried to help and even sought the help of an organization that specialized in what was troubling us. But nothing worked. Soon, the money we had put away for retirement began to disappear, and we had to struggle with credit card debts. Mired in bankruptcy, in December 1992, we decided to separate. We had managed to sell the mobile home in 1986 and had bought another house. Now, facing divorce, we decided to sell it and split the profits. Nina rented an apartment for herself, and we worked together to prepare our furniture and appliances for an auction, hoping to get some money from the sale of our belongings.

That fall, I had been forced to quit my job at Baldinger Baking Company. Through the years I had undergone several surgeries to repair injuries. The final blows that ended my work there were a torn rotator cuff and the surgery that followed. So, supported by disability pay, in the middle of a separation heading for divorce, and preparing to say Goodbye to my dream retirement house, I had each day all to myself as I was dealing with all my worldly possessions—packing some and marking others to be sold.

About a week before the auction, I had a whole afternoon alone in the house and no agenda. I wandered past the tagged refrigerator, couches, and television—all symbols of the life Nina and I had built and shared together for more than twenty years. Then I decided to sort through my library—a couple of shelves stuffed full of the books I had collected through the years. I would keep only the most precious ones. Starting in the upper left corner, I sifted through them, smiling at familiar old titles and frowning in consternation when I found ones I didn't even remember I owned. Most of these books ended up in boxes to go to the auctioneer.

Then, my fingers snagged a book my sister Friedl had sent me years before. It was *The Great Controversy,* which was written by Ellen G. White and published by the Seventh-day Adventist Church. When it came in the mail, I shoved it behind my other books, where it gathered dust. I loved my sister dearly but had never wanted to get near the crazy ideas of what I called her "sect."

I was ready to toss the book in one of the boxes of rejects, but something tugged at my heart. Friedl had passed away two years before after several strokes weakened her body, and touching the book she had sent me made me feel sentimental. I thumbed through the pages idly, scanning the chapter titles but not reading much of the text. Then I noticed that some chapters were about what would happen in the future, and I started to get interested in the prophecies. With a long winter afternoon stretching before me and no one to look forward to at the end of it, I started at the book's beginning. The rest of the books could wait to be organized another day—I had a week before the auctioneer was to come.

As I began to read, I was immediately touched by the tenderness with which the author described Jesus. She said that He wept for the people of Jerusalem and that even though they sinned, He persisted in giving them every chance to be saved.

When I read that the seventh day is the sacred Sabbath, I realized that even at those times when I tried to live a moral life and follow the Ten Commandments, I still had broken the fourth one—I hadn't kept the day of rest God gave His children to remember Him by. I also read of the importance of tithing as a sign of our commitment to God—that we realize we should follow His commandments in response to His love.

And when I read what Ellen White wrote about the state of people in death, I was amazed. My whole life I had struggled with the idea of hell. It made no sense to me that Cain, who murdered only his brother, had already suffered the fires of hell for six thousand years, while Hitler, who was responsible for the deaths of millions, had been burning for only fifty years. (Several years after the war, I had come to realize the truly evil things Hitler had done.) In other words, Cain, the lesser sinner, would be punished—tormented—six thousand years longer than Hitler, the greater sinner. How about Satan? All the sinners who have died have gotten a head start on him when he should have the longest sentence of all. And what about some kid who stole a candy bar and then died before he had the chance to repent? Did he have to suffer the same punishment as the Hitlers of the world?

In *The Great Controversy,* I found the first explanation of death that I'd ever heard that matched the idea of a loving God. In chapter 34, I read, "The Bible declares that the dead know not anything, that their thoughts have perished; they have no part in anything that is done under the sun; they know nothing of the joys or sorrows of those who were dearest to them on earth."* Now this was a God of love. Instead of hurling those who had sinned to eternal suffering, He let them go to sleep to spend eternity dead, away from His presence—not alive in eternal pain. God didn't find pleasure in watching the people He created twist in agony!

All these teachings appealed to my head—they made sense to me. But when I read the chapter "Facing Life's Record," my heart was pulled from the grip of coldness that had held it for forty-seven years. I was pacing in the living room as I read it,

---

* Ellen G. White, *The Great Controversy* (Mountain View, Calif.: Pacific Press®, 1950), 556.

not wanting to put the book down but tired of sitting. That chapter explains that all those who confess their sins will have them blotted out from God's record, and they will be invited into eternal life—treated as if they had never sinned! Ellen White describes the scene in front of God's throne:

> While Jesus is pleading for the subjects of His grace, Satan accuses them before God as transgressors. The great deceiver has sought to lead them into skepticism, to cause them to lose confidence in God, to separate themselves from His love, and to break His law. Now he points to the record of their lives, to the defects of character, the unlikeness to Christ . . . and . . . he claims them as his subjects.
>
> Jesus does not excuse their sins, but shows their penitence and faith, and, claiming for them forgiveness, He lifts His wounded hands before the Father and the holy angels, saying: I know them by name. I have graven them on the palms of My hands.*

A little further down, she quotes Revelation 3:4: "They shall walk with Me in white, for they are worthy." That line echoed and re-echoed in my thoughts. I had spent my entire life believing I was unworthy—that I could never be good enough for God. First, it was the mud I got on my pants when I was a little boy and later, my life of infidelity. I thought my failings, my sins, made me too dirty to be loved by the condemning Christ who stared at me from the living-room wall. But now, at the age of sixty-two, in the living room that was about to be sold because of another failed relationship, I read that Christ was

---

* White, *The Great Controversy*, 484.

offering His wounds to make me—*me*—as white as snow.

For so many years, I had strived to make myself a good person. I knew that as far as God was concerned I was lost, but I thought that at least in this present world I could redeem myself with a good life. I ran away from Germany to become successful in America. I married Olga to become a family man, only to destroy that relationship with my weak selfishness. I joined a church to make my family OK, only to have my children run away from home and my marriage fall apart. My career had been ended by injury, and now my dream house would be sold at below-market value.

I stood in my living room among the boxes of books and thought, *I can't hold onto anything I've worked for. It just runs through my fingers like water.* I stood there dumbfounded. I couldn't hold on to anything. I was alone with no one to call.

All my life, I ran away each time the dreams I built crumbled. Now, I had a choice to make. When our marriage ended and I had no material things left, I could run away again and leave my children and Nina and start all over. But experience had taught me that would only mask my problems for so long. My other choice was to surrender to the God who offered me a clean slate and the tools to build a solid life in Him. As His undeserved, unconditional love found its way into my heart for the first time, I bowed my head. "Lord," I prayed, "have it Your way from now on. I make a mess of everything I do on my own. I want You to have my life." And then I promised God that, with His help, I would keep the seventh day as the Sabbath and be faithful in my tithe.

In the days that followed, an image came into my head over and over. I saw Jesus lifting His wounded hands to the Father and telling Him I was carved in them. This living image replaced the condemning picture of Christ that I had carried from my home in Sprottau.

I also realized that I could confess my sins to God and let Him erase them, and so, with tears flowing and my heart aching with the memory of each sin, I named them to God one by one. "I betrayed Olga and Udo and Nora, Father. I am so sorry. I pretended to follow You in Norfolk when it was all a show. Forgive my hypocrisy, God."

There were sins that had made my stomach sick for years each time I thought of them. I spoke each of these to God and asked Him to forgive me, and with each one I named, my heart felt lighter and my tears flowed more freely. "Forgive me for treating Nina and the kids so meanly when they were little. Thank You for forgiving me."

As I confessed my sins and crossed them off the list in my head, my tears of sorrow and regret became tears of thankfulness to a God who was taking the burdens I had carried for so many years. When I drifted off to sleep that night, such a heavy stone had been rolled off my heart that I felt almost as if I were floating.

The next day, I called my niece Anita, Friedl's daughter, to share my newfound faith. I told her that *The Great Controversy* showed me God's love and convinced me of the importance of His commands. When Anita finally spoke, I heard tears in her voice. "Uncle Waldy," she said, "I am so happy for you. I just wish Mom had lived to see this. She fasted for you every day your mother did, from the day you left Germany until she died, and I know she prayed that you would find this peace."

I hadn't known that Friedl had fasted for me all those years, but I know now that the prayers she and Mama prayed and the fasting they did had something to do with the Holy Spirit's persistence in my life. They never gave up on me, so He never did.

The first Saturday after my living-room experience, I woke up resolved to keep the Sabbath and refrain from work. I fixed myself breakfast and then sat and stared at the wall. *What do you do on a day when you can't work?* I thought. *I guess you go shopping.* So, to keep my first Sabbath, I went shopping. I started my journey with wobbling steps!

The next Sabbath, I went shopping again, but then I began to realize that while I wasn't working, the people who were selling me things were. *What do you do on a day when you can't do anything?* I wondered. I started brainstorming about other restful activities and then found a good church family at the Capital City Seventh-day Adventist school in Maplewood, Minnesota. They taught me a lot more about biblical doctrines, and they showed me Adventist traditions that make the Sabbath a joy.

The following months were difficult. When I had to move out of the house, I had only our rusted-out VW Campmobile, which needed a complete engine overhaul. With the generosity of friends who were helping me while I got back on my feet, I eventually was able to rent an apartment in St. Paul, which I furnished with four chairs and a table from a secondhand store. I slept on a twenty-dollar air mattress and used big boxes covered with old bed sheets to serve as other furniture. For several months, I had less than one hundred dollars with which to buy food and necessities, and sometimes I sat down at the dinner table with just a piece of bread, a stalk of celery, and a glass of water. But I thanked God for providing that food. During all

this time, as a man of sixty-two who could have been heartbro-
ken because he'd lost all the funds for his retirement, I felt at
peace knowing that I had God with me. Because of His presence, for the first time in my life I wasn't afraid of the future.

With some odd jobs and back pay for three years of wages
I'd lost because of my disability, I slowly got back on my feet.
I was able to afford a trip back to Germany in 1993. For the
first time since rushing away on that February morning almost
fifty years before, I returned to Sprottau (now called Szprotawa).
Walking on the freshly fallen snow, I felt like a kid again, with
a lightness I never thought possible. The roads and Sprotte River
and old buildings were made beautiful by glistening white
snow. They were clean. They were my same old friends even
though the war and fifty years of life had battered and aged
them and given them a new name in a foreign tongue. They still
stood, ready for a new day.

CHAPTER TWELVE

On the Bridge

Six years after my trip to Germany, I am back in Europe again—this time in the enemy's territory, England. I stand in the metal-sided telegraph room of HMS *Belfast*. It is cold. Part of my growth over the last seven years has been to extend the forgiveness God gave me to the people who have wronged me. I thought I had dealt with that. But as I stand in the bowels of this English battleship, I tremble with anger and with hatred for each person in this country. They're all responsible for my brothers' deaths. A whole country of people—unforgiven in my heart.

It has been fifty-five years since Erwin sank in the English Channel, but as I stand behind the mannequin in the decoding seat with my fists tightened to still my trembling fingers, I wish with all my heart that my brother would walk around the corner and step into the room to entertain me with one of his stories. I feel as if he might, as if I lost him just yesterday—as most people must feel in the days after they lose a loved one. I half expect a tall, handsome, strong young man to walk into the room and put his hand on my shoulder and tell me that everything is all right.

But that won't happen. These Tommies—they stole him from me.

I shake my head. *It's all over,* I tell myself. *This ended years ago. We aren't enemies anymore and never should have been.* But no matter how often I say this, my heart continues to pound harder, and I feel as if I will burst with either sorrow or anger.

"Erwin, come back," the child voice inside my head cries as I look around the room. I want my big brother. I feel my heart sink deep at the loss—the loss I have never let surface until now, the words I have never spoken, the words that were trapped inside me when I was fourteen years old. And the next second I'm thinking, *I'll fight them. I'll get them back for what they did to you, Erwin—for what they took from me.*

I hate them. I hate them all, the whole country, and I'm alarmed by this blackness that's growing in my heart. I thought Jesus had taken it away.

I look at the back of the head of the dummy sitting in a chair that's probably just like the one where Erwin spent his last days—sitting where the man mirroring Erwin on the British side of the war sat while the two ships shot at each other and traded young life for young life after young life. I imagine Erwin's body flung overboard in the fighting, the cold water of the English Channel clutching his body, tugging it down, forcing the life out of him, burying him under the heavy water.

A tear rolls down my cheek. The dam is about to burst. I have to breathe deeply to get air to my lungs through the tight knot in my throat.

Clang, clang, clang. Many feet pound down the metal stairs. I wipe my cheek dry. A big group of people will be here at any second. I can tell from the accents it is a group of American tourists, loud and boisterous. I don't want them to see my tears.

The words from the telegram addressed to my parents announcing Erwin's death echo in my head: "Your dear son found his grave in the waters of the English Channel." My brave, strong brother. I have never seen his grave. I wanted to be smart like him, to know the things he did. I never got to say Goodbye. I never got to toss a handful of dirt into his grave and set flowers by a marker to honor his resting place.

Suddenly, I know what I have to do. I rush out of the room and up the stairs, brushing past the Americans, my head down. I still have tears in my eyes, but I feel the ache in my heart beginning to crack, anticipation of release beginning to seep through.

I climb the four flights of stairs, up past the weapons rooms and officers' quarters and the rooms where the course of battles was decided, out of the musty metal maze to the open air, where the sunlight has turned golden and falls around the ship and the city.

I'm not thinking about the British right now. I'm thinking of Erwin, remembering how he used to chase me around the yard when he came home for a holiday, the way he closed his eyes when he played the violin, how he drew the bow across the strings in harmony with Mama's voice, remembering how I never got to say Goodbye, wishing he were here beside me.

My nose is running now, as are my eyes, and I sniffle past the people on the street, rushing west along the river, following its curve past ancient buildings that have seen more wars than even I. Oh, how I hate wars. How I wish I could reverse time and do something to these British, destroy them first, so they couldn't destroy my family.

I'm walking fast now, my eyes peeled, looking for something as sharply as I can through the cloudy tears. I know what I need to find.

I want all these people to go away. I want them all to disappear, I want it to be just me and God and this river and—

Ah ha! There it is.

I'm out of breath and shaken, but I don't stop. I run across the street and find myself standing in front of a small flower shop that's just about to close. The shopkeeper is rolling his outdoor display carts inside. I don't make eye contact with him.

Taking a deep breath, I catch the door before it closes and go inside. The smell of many flowers fills my nostrils. Even at the end of the day, they are bright and beautiful and solemn, a great amount of God's beauty captured in each small grouping.

I walk along the row of bouquets, the scent tingling inside my nose. I scan past the too-cheerful yellow and pink bouquets. *What will speak of Erwin? What will honor who he was?* Then a splash of blue catches my eye—a large bouquet standing in the back, almost completely hidden behind a loud, exotic bouquet of hot pink tiger lilies. That's the one. Those are the flowers for Erwin.

The blue cornflower—the national flower of Germany—has made it into this London flower shop. Each stalk holds a dozen or more individual flowers, making a choir of little blue trumpets, and there are fourteen or fifteen of the stalks in the bouquet. The blue reminds me of the tears I've held inside my heart and the sea that holds Erwin's body. Scattered in the blue field of cornflowers are roses, some white, some crimson red—purity and honor and innocence and love and blood. I lift the bouquet from behind the others and pay the shopkeeper his price, never making eye contact. My heart just beats with thoughts of Erwin now.

I rush outside and continue along the river until I see the next bridge: the Waterloo. As I turn onto the bridge and head over the water, I walk more slowly and hold the flowers close to my chin, drinking in their colors. As I walk, I look to my left. The buildings of Parliament are silhouetted against the sky, and as the sun sinks behind them, it lights up slivers of cloud above the buildings, soft pink against the deepening blue of the sky.

Now I'm at the middle of the bridge. I turn to the east, toward Germany, toward the English Channel, toward the radar towers and guns of HMS *Belfast,* and look down to the dark waters of the Thames, where ripples flash a light blue and pink, reflecting the sky. The river is wide here—a wide, slow, lazy flow in the middle of a bustling city.

I feel people walking past me, but they don't matter. All that matters is that I am under this sky with my God looking down on me, that I'm standing over the waters that eventually will flow over my brother's body—over the bodies of all the men who fell in that battle.

My dear heavenly Father . . .

That's all the prayer I can squeeze out; the only requiem I can say for my brother, my cheeks now wet with tears. I draw the bouquet to my nose and smell the red rose in the center, a deep breath in with my eyes closed, squeezing tears out, an old man with wrinkles and no hair grieving the loss of his brother, feeling the wound in my heart as if it had been made yesterday. Then I open my eyes and toss the bouquet out from the bridge. I watch it fall to the water and float, taken up by the great current.

The river is moving faster than it appeared to be before I threw the bouquet. The flowers coast past the buildings and debris on the shore, and I watch them, tears streaming silently down my face. *Goodbye, Erwin. May you rest in peace, my brother. May I see you on the resurrection day.*

Tears flow out of the lump in my throat and through my eyes and wash down my cheeks—wash away the loss of my brother, wash the grief out of a place that has not opened up in all my sixty-eight years, letting him go, letting the tears go that never before fell for him or for Manfred or Walter or Edmund. As I let my tears go, I also let Erwin go. And as I let Erwin go, I let my past go—let go of the blows I have been dealt by the Enemy from the moment this war began.

I stand like that for many minutes, focusing on the bouquet until the last dots of bobbing red and white roses fade into the fast-falling dusk. I hope the flowers will float all night and reach the English Channel to settle with Erwin.

My tears are slowing, a soft breeze off the water brushing them dry on my cheeks. I take in a deep breath and sigh, the air shuddering on the way out.

Goodbye.

It's getting colder. I put my hands in my pockets, unwilling to move my feet, and I watch the spot on the river where I last saw the bouquet.

For all these years, I have carried the hatred deep in my heart because of how the war tore up my family. Even those of us who didn't die have lived the rest of our lives with wounds— my brother Kurt with a limp from his leg wound, me with my shattered dreams. When we fled from Sprottau, my life ceased to be shaped by my wishes and was jostled instead by the simple desire to avoid hunger. The bomb in the train station in Goerlitz froze my heart and stole my emotions. For too many years I strove just to feed my hungry body and soul.

But now—now I can breathe again. I can cry. I can feel. And I see that the war took the lives not only of my countrymen but of the British, of Americans, of Russians, of Africans and Filipinos and Italians and Japanese. Almost fifty million people erased from the earth, erased from their families.

I turn my feet in the direction of my hotel, and as I move into the light of a streetlamp, I pass two British women walking the other direction and chatting furiously with each other. One of them is telling the other the story of some new romance, the other asking questions with a shrill excitement, and I feel the corner of my mouth twitch, threatening a smile.

This is strange. I don't feel an ounce of anger.

I step out of the lamplight and pass back into the dimness of early night. Under the next lamp, I glimpse a middle-aged man and his teenage daughter talking quietly, keys jangling in one of his hands, his other hand on her shoulder. I find myself nodding to him as we catch each other's eyes before passing back into darkness.

I walk through the light of streetlamp after streetlamp, and with each human being who passes me, my heart leaps a little. It is lighter than it has felt in years. I thought it felt light when I asked God to forgive my sins, but that was nothing. I am floating now.

Oh, God, I forgive them! The words leap into my mind.

That's it. I forgive them.

I stop in my tracks. I've forgiven them, and that has set me free. People look like people again. No longer the enemy, they are my brothers and sisters. I'd like to hear that man's story, that woman's. I wish I could share a cup of tea with that gentleman with the mustache. I'm sure we could tell each other stories of losing our families, of what it took to recover. I am free to love them.

I resume my walk, passing from pool of light to pool of light. I head toward a warm dinner and bed, and all the while the bouquet is making its way out to the sea. And I remember,

> He will again have compassion on us,
> And will subdue our iniquities.
> You will cast all our sins
> Into the depths of the sea (Micah 7:19).

All our sins together, cast into the depths, ending the war within.

Epilogue

Since that day on the Waterloo Bridge, I have traveled many more miles. I've moved between Minnesota and California several times and traveled all over the States and through Germany and Mexico and back to Minnesota. In my retirement, I still pedal my bicycle fifty miles on days when I have the energy. When people hear my life story and say that it seems I was running from things my whole life, I joke that at the age of seventy-nine, I'm still running. The difference is that now I'm not running away—I have God right with me every step.

I officially joined the Seventh-day Adventist Church by profession of faith in 2004. Accepting Jesus' love for me hasn't made me perfect by any means. I still struggle with being aggressively ambitious. But I've learned that I don't have to pedal myself to the top of each mountain now: God takes care of my needs. I also struggle with criticizing people who act differently than me, but I have started to catch myself at that and realize it isn't my position to judge. Each day, I strive to see people the way God sees them. I've had family struggles in the years since my living-room conversion—Nina and I tried to make a go of being married again after our first divorce. But the same problems persisted, and I came home one day to find she had left for good.

Even with that disappointment, though, God has given me many triumphs. I was able to ask and receive Olga's forgiveness before she passed away in 2002. I spent more than a year with Kurt in Germany before he died in 2005. Though we had very different temperaments, we cared for each other as brothers, and by taking care of him in some of his last days, I was able to thank him for the care he gave our parents in their old age.

I am blessed to keep in touch with all of my children. I have apologized that I wasn't the kind of father I should have been when they were little, and I strive to be what they need now. Udo and his wife, Patty, own their own business in California and attend a community church with their children AJ and Simon. Nora lives in New York and is a real-estate agent. Edmund has given me six grandchildren: Erik, who is in the U.S. Navy; Nathan; Kayla; Edmund Jr.; Allison; and Derek. Edmund and his wife, Kari, live in Minnesota. Rhonda has a son, Travis, who will graduate from high school next year, and she works hard at her job with the airlines. She, Travis, and her husband, Todd, live in Minnesota as well. In addition to my children and grandchildren, I have been given a spiritual family in the Adventist community wherever I go in the world.

Even now, the blessing that my Lutheran pastor in Bavaria gave me echoes in my head—the verse he gave me from his deathbed:

Then Jesus said to the twelve, "Do you also want to go away?"

But Simon Peter answered Him, "Lord, to whom shall we go? You have the words of eternal life. Also we have come to believe and know that You are the Christ, the Son of the living God" (John 6:67–69).

God has guided me through each experience of my life to the realization that Jesus Christ is the only One in the world who offers the words of eternal life. No one else and nothing else does. I no longer carry in my head the picture of the stern, condemning Christ that hung in my home in Germany. Nor am I stuck with the elitist, distant Christ of the Nazi regime. It has taken many struggles, many days of running and of stumbling in darkness to get where I am today. But my Father led me through them all to the day when I met the Son of the living God and fell on my knees. The heavenly Father has revealed the true Jesus, who lifts His wounded hands before the Father and the holy angels and says, I know Waldemar by name. I have graven him on the palms of My hands.

Now I have nothing to hide. Each day, God is melting the icy walls of my selfish disposition ever so slowly and is replacing my heart of stone with a heart of flesh. He leads me into an abundant life—one that I yearned for but couldn't find after the explosion at the train station numbed my heart. Now I understand that I don't earn my salvation by trying to keep God's law, but I can show my love to Him by seeking to follow His instructions. Now, every day is new for me. Jesus' precious blood erases yesterday's mistakes, and I know that the Son of the living God loves me, the worst of sinners. Living each day knowing that He forgives me and loves me satisfies my deepest hunger.

May He find me loving Him until I take my last breath. May I go to sleep with Christ in my heart, and when He comes again, may I wake up to spend eternity with Him.

My wish is for you to be there too.

Therese Leonhardt (Mama)

Albert Leonhardt (Papa)

Waldemar's birthplace in Sprottau

Olga, Waldemar, and Udo, 1961

A passport photo, 1980s

Edmund, Nina, and
Rhonda, 1980

Nora and Waldemar, 1995

Waldemar and Udo, 2003

Rhonda and Waldemar, 2003

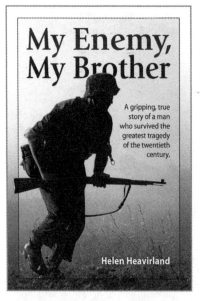